HOW TO SAVE THE WHOLE STINKIN' PLANET

HOW TO SAVE THE WHOLE STINKIN' PLANET

LEE CONSTABLE

Illustrated by JAMES HART

PUFFIN BOOKS

PUFFIN BOOKS

UK | USA | Canada | Ireland | Australia
India | New Zealand | South Africa | China

Penguin Random House Australia is part of the Penguin Random House group of
companies whose addresses can be found at global.penguinrandomhouse.com.

First published by Puffin Books, an imprint of
Penguin Random House Australia Pty Ltd, in 2019

Cover and internal illustrations by James Hart
Cover design by Bruno Herfst and Marina Messiha
© Penguin Random House Australia Pty Ltd
Typeset in Gill Sans by Midland Typesetters, Australia

Printed and bound in Australia by Griffin Press, part of Ovato, an accredited
ISO AS/NZS 14001 Environmental Management Systems printer

A catalogue record for this
book is available from the
National Library of Australia

ISBN 978 1 76 089026 1 (Paperback)

Penguin Random House Australia uses papers that are natural and recyclable
products, made from wood grown in sustainable forests. The logging and
manufacture processes are expected to conform to the environmental
regulations of the country of origin.

penguin.com.au

Credits for line and border design elements:
Varlamova Lydmila/Shutterstock; Nikolaeva/
Shutterstock; olnik_y/Shutterstock; my.skills/
Shutterstock

To the next generation of eco-heroes standing up for the future of our whole stinkin' planet.

You are my heroes.

CONTENTS

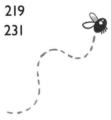

So you want to save the whole stinkin' planet? You're not alone. But what does the planet need saving from? WHY is it such a stinkin' problem? And what can *you* do?

What STINKS?

We have a lot to thank the planet for. The planet provides us with electricity to run our technology, fuel to power our cars, water to drink and grow our food, and all the things we need to make everything from buildings to clothing to toys. But over time, we've been taking more and more from the planet and the planet has been getting some pretty gross gifts from us in return. Pollution, fresh water shortages and habitat destruction are just a handful of the mean things we're giving our old pal. It's just not fair! In fact, it straight up STINKS.

We've been causing a stink and letting off some nasty gases in the process. When we burn coal to make electricity and burn fuel to power our cars, we let gases float into the atmosphere. They're called GREENHOUSE GASES because they trap heat in like a greenhouse does. CARBON DIOXIDE (CO_2) and METHANE are just two examples of these gases. By trapping heat in, they affect the overall temperature of our planet and over the years the temperature has been going up! This has changed our weather systems and our climate.

8

Climate is the description of the weather conditions we experience over a long period of time. Take a look outside, what's the weather like right now? Sunny? Cloudy? Rainy? Windy? Hot? Cold?

Even though we get cold or hot, rainy or sunny weather, overall, the climate has been changing a lot. And our planet has been feeling this in a big way.

What can YOU do?

There are loads of ways that eco-heroes like you can help to SAVE THE WHOLE STINKIN' PLANET!

- You could volunteer to help protect an endangered animal
- You could plant trees that breathe in CO_2
- You could use solar energy (energy from the sun) to power your electronics instead of getting electricity from burning coal
- You could be careful with how much water and electricity you use so it doesn't go to waste

But there's one thing you probably do every single day without even thinking twice about it. You put something in the bin! Thinking about where our WASTE goes and making the best bin-based decisions we can, goes a long way towards taking the pressure off our poor old planet.

That's where I come in. My name is CAPTAIN GARBOLOGY and I'm about to take you on a **garbological adventure**! We are going to get into the gory details of our waste and figure out how it harms our planet and what WE can do to change that. First, let's see what the problem is.

What's the big stinkin' problem with waste?
Humans produce around 2 BILLION TONNES of rubbish a year!

How heavy is that? Let's compare it to some big, heavy stuff from cities around the world.

2 BILLION TONNES is as heavy as . . .

350 Great Pyramids of Giza
80,000 Statues of Liberty
200,000 Eiffel Towers
37,900 Sydney Harbour Bridges

That's a lot! And if we don't change our ways, we will produce even more rubbish as time goes on.

So how does rubbish hurt the planet?

Lots of things that could be recycled DON'T get recycled which hurts our planet in many ways:

- Not recycling our rubbish means we keep taking more and more from the planet so we can make things from scratch.
- When the waste we don't recycle breaks down it produces greenhouse gases like methane that add to that big <u>CLIMATE CHANGE</u> problem!
- A lot of our rubbish also ends up littering the land, waterways and oceans, harming our wildlife and their habitats too.

The good news is, there's a lot we can do to change this and help our planet get back to good health. You can join me and train to become a **WASTE WARRIOR!**

Are you up to the challenge? Then read on!

Captain Garbology

WELCOME TO WASTE WARRIOR TRAINING

HIYA!
I'm Captain Garbology.

Hello future Waste Warrior!

Welcome to Waste Warrior Training. You've got an important mission ahead and if you succeed, you'll be a Waste Warrior just like me.

That's me, over there . . . in the cape.

If you think my name sounds super weird, and you're wondering what on earth it means, then feast your peepers on this fancy dictionary definition . . .

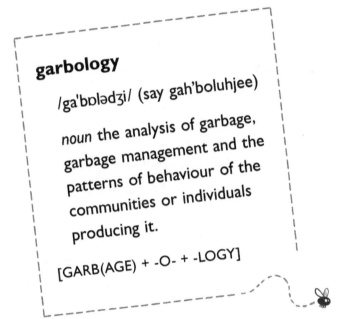

garbology

/gaˈbɒlədʒi/ (say gah'boluhjee)

noun the analysis of garbage, garbage management and the patterns of behaviour of the communities or individuals producing it.

[GARB(AGE) + -O- + -LOGY]

I know, right! Garbology is seriously cool and mega important when it comes to SAVING THE WHOLE STINKIN' PLANET!

So, what's our mission?

NAME: MISSION GARBOLOGY

DETAILS: Our mission is to save the whole stinkin' planet by getting skilled-up and clued-in on all things waste so we can share our wisdom with everyone!

First, you need to find out where all your waste goes after you throw it away and how you can make sure it goes to the best place possible.

Along the way you will get hands-on with DIY activities, get to grips with the wonderful waste science of garbology and earn badges that will add up to make you a WASTE WARRIOR!

As a Waste Warrior, you can use all the knowledge and skills you have learnt to help heal our planet and make it less stinky.

HOW TO USE THIS BOOK

This book is your guide through each stage of the mission. In every chapter you will follow a different journey that your rubbish could take. Some of these quests are fast-paced, some are smelly and some paths will work better for some types of rubbish than others!

Your Waste Warrior training has been broken down into the following sections:

LET'S GET GARBOLOGICAL

These sections will bring you up to speed with the science behind the garbage and how it relates to the whole stinkin' planet.

GET HANDS-ON

These sections give you an opportunity to put garbology into action with DIY activities.

THE BIG STINK SHRINK-DOWN

This is where you will experience your rubbish up close and in gross detail. We will be shrinking down and diving in to go on a journey with our junk like never before!

FOUL FACTS

Throughout this adventure I will share some of my favourite garbological facts. They'll draw you in and gross you out. Soon you will be able to impress your mates with your Waste Warrior knowledge. YOU. ARE. WELCOME.

THE RUBBISH ROUND-UP

We're putting the QUEST in questions! At the end of each chapter you'll have a chance to put your new skills and know-how to the test. If you ace the answers you'll receive a badge and advance to the next stage of the mission.

To be successful in this garbological mission to save the whole stinkin' planet, you will need:

A Garbology Lab Book

This can be any old notebook. It's a place where you can make notes, complete fun activities and record your hands-on garbology experiments.

A Grossary

If you see a word that looks like THIS and you aren't sure what it means, flip to the back of the book where you can learn all about it.

Imagination

You'll have to have an open mind if you want to shrink down and be at one with your waste in new ways throughout this journey. You might want to imagine yourself up a pair of bin boots and a face mask too, just to be safe.

Curiosity

Never stop asking questions and looking for answers. Make sure you jot down all the questions you have in your Garbology Lab Book.

GARBOLOGY
RECRUIT NAME
101

Before we embark on our garbological adventure, you need a Waste Warrior recruit name. The first letter of your name and your birth month will reveal your name.

A - The Magnificent	**N** – The Spontaneous
B – The Fantastic	**O** – The Elusive
C – The Wonderful	**P** – The Fabulous
D – The Epic	**Q** – The Unforgettable
E – The Great	**R** – The Inquisitive
F – The Unpredictable	**S** – The Amazing
G – The Brilliant	**T** – The Spectacular
H – The Unbeatable	**U** – The Inspirational
I – The Terrific	**V** – The Brave
J – The Curious	**W** – The Awesome
K – The Incredible	**X** – The Super
L – The Mysterious	**Y** – The Strong
M – The Fearless	**Z** – The Unbelievable

January – Stinko	**July – Ewwwwwwwwww**
February – Grossio	**August – Splatto**
March – Yuck-Yuck	**September – Icky-Sticky**
April – Disgusto	**October – Rot-a-Lot**
May – Revoltron	**November – Ooey-Gooey**
June – Smelliosa	**December – Gassius**

WASTE WARRIOR TRAINING ID

Now you've got your recruit name sorted, you'll need to make your Waste Warrior ID card. Here's mine . . .

DEPARTMENT OF GARBOLOGY

WASTE WARRIOR ID CARD

CAPTAIN GARBOLOGY

Special powers: Can make the grossest things fun

Things I throw out the most: Bin boots! Sliding down rubbish piles and leaping through bin juice sure is tough on my footwear

Things I like to reuse/recycle: Anything and everything I can

Favourite smell: Vanilla

LEAST favourite smell: Bin juice

I carry my ID card with me wherever I go. You never know when you might need it for official planet saving business.

In your <u>Garbology Lab Book</u> design your own ID card. Make sure you include your answers to these essential planet saving questions!

Recruit name: *(e.g. The Great Disgusto)*

Special powers: *(e.g. Can withstand the stinkiest stenches)*

Things I throw out the most:

Things I like to reuse/recycle:

Favourite smell:

LEAST favourite smell:

Now you're ready to get started. Put that curiosity cap on, shift your brain into gear and let's go!

CHAPTER ONE

GET IN
THE BIN!

Have you ever thought about what happened to all the things you've thrown away? Can you remember everything you've put in the bin today? This week? What about in your WHOLE LIFE?

Where did that banana skin go after you tossed it on the walk to school? What's the yoghurt container from recess last week up to now? Did your old, holey footy socks end up somewhere nice when you finally listened to Mum and chucked them out?

Did you stop to wonder what journey *any* of your rubbish went on after you threw it away?

Hmmm . . . Didn't think so!

If you want to be a Waste Warrior you need to get clued-up and rubbish ready. That's why I'm here – Captain Garbology – your friendly neighbourhood eco-hero, ready to get your brain into garbological gear.

Our first port of call is the common household bin; this is where our garbological adventure starts. Not to worry, brave recruit, you don't have to travel far for your first day of training – just head to the kitchen and flip open that bin.

The things we throw away every day don't just disappear. Nope – they go on a **JOURNEY**!

This can be a journey of being reused. It could be a journey of breaking down and becoming something new. OR it could be a **stinky, yucky, smelly** journey that ends up hurting the planet we love.

This chapter is all about getting up close and personal with the rubbish in your bin. WHY? Simple! Once we know what our rubbish is made from, we can figure out what to do with it and make sure it doesn't end up hurting our planet. After all, it's *your* bin and *your* choice what journey your leftover vegemite sandwich crust goes on.

So, we're shrinking down, getting in the bin and going on a sometimes gross, but always engrossing journey with our rubbish.

SKILLS TO MASTER

If you don't get the basics right, you won't be able to even begin saving the whole stinkin' planet!

In this chapter you'll learn:
- What's in your bin
- How to sort waste into different types
- The difference between hard and soft plastic
- Which wheelie bin to use

BRAIN STARTERS

Let's get straight to the **NITTY-GRITTY, STINKY-STICKY**!
As my newest recruit, I have a few questions for you. Write the
answers in your <u>Garbology Lab Book</u>.

If you don't know all the answers, that's okay! By the end of
your training you'll know every single one and have lots of new
questions you've never even thought of before.

1. **What was the last thing you threw away?**
   (draw what it was)

2. **What was it made of?**
   *(e.g. plastic, paper, metal, glass . . .? Maybe it's made
   of more than one thing)*

3. **Which bin did it go in?**
   (general waste, recycling, compost, other)

4. **Where does it go next?**

5. **What happens then?**
   *(draw a picture of where you imagine your rubbish
   ends up and what happens to it when it gets there)*

FOUL FACTS

Waste comes from lots of different places. It comes from constructing and demolishing buildings and roads, from factories, from mines and from power plants that make electricity . . . And that's only a few examples!

So how much of that **2 BILLION** tonnes (37,900 Sydney Harbour Bridges) of planet-wide yearly waste do YOU throw away?

Australians chuck 261 Sydney Harbour Bridges – or 13.8 million tonnes – worth of junk a year into the bins in our streets, schools and homes. That's around 560 kilograms per person, which is equal to the weight of a dairy cow! That's a lot for one person to chuck.

THE **BIG STINK** SHRINK-DOWN

It's time, brave recruit, to power up our imaginations, put aside our fears, pull on our bin boots and jump right into the **ICKY-STICKY, OOEY-GOOEY, RANKY-STANKY** details. I'll use my powers to shrink you down and get you to the first stage of our mission.

Let's lift the lid.

It's time to . . .

GET IN THE BIN!

Well, yes, of course I'm serious.

Do you smell that? Breathe it in,

recruit, and try not to gag . . .

Yes, it's the smell of rubbish, but it's also the smell of ADVENTURE! Follow me.

Here we GOOOOOOOO!

Sliding down the plastic packaging . . .

Squeezing past the cereal box . . .

Crashing into the plastic bottles . . .

And finally, here we are . . .

Squelching through the bin juice.

Bin juice means we've made it to the heart of this STINKY STENCH FEST – the bottom of the bin!

Now we're here, let me fill you in on some FILTHY FACTS.

LET'S GET GARBOLOGICAL

Why should we care so **stinkin'** much about **smelly** old garbage? Just put it in the bin and out of your mind, right?

Let's start with what we just saw and **smelt** in shrink-down mode. The stank and the bin juice tells us that your rubbish has already started to break down or DECOMPOSE. This means it's breaking down into smaller and smaller parts thanks to all the MICROBES eating the edible bits!

In nature there's no such thing as waste. A tree falls and microbes in the soil break it down. Other plants live on it and the NUTRIENTS from the tree return to the soil and allow new microbes to thrive and new plants to grow. When an animal dies it becomes food for other animals and microbes that break it down too. The poop from the animals and microbes goes into the soil, plants can eat these nutrients, animals can eat these plants, and it goes on and on.

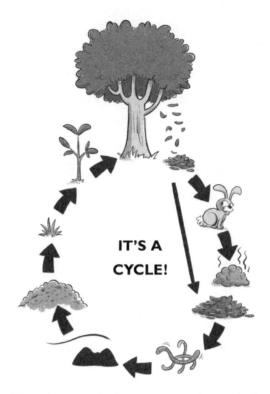

IT'S A CYCLE!

There's no such thing as waste in nature!

Not all microbes are the same. The community of microbes living in your soil are very different to the population of microbes in your bin. Different microbes will break things down in different ways! We Waste Warriors want to encourage microbes that are going to break down our waste without adding to the big stinkin' problem by making greenhouse gases. We'll meet more of the microbes we want on our team later in your training on **page 144**.

So nature is awesome when it comes to getting rid of its waste. But, unlike nature, us humans create things that are not made to be used forever and which don't always break down to become something new.

The story of our unwanted waste doesn't end at the bin. In fact, some of it doesn't even make it *to* the bin! Our waste can end up littering the environment around us. It might even get into stormwater drains and wash out to sea where marine animals might try to eat it or get caught in it!

To tackle this problem we have to not only put our rubbish in the bin, but we have to know what we're dealing with and where it should go!

Our rubbish could go to **landfill**, be **recycled**, be **composted** or even be **reused**. And it's a Waste Warrior's job to know these options inside out and back-to-front so that we can make the best decisions for our planet.

But, my eager recruit, studying the theory of garbology is just **one** part of your training, the other part is to GET HANDS-ON!

GET HANDS-ON

MAKE YOUR VERY OWN PONG PIE!

Before we figure out what to **do** with our waste, we need to know what sort of waste we're dealing with. This activity will help you sort your waste into different types and see whether there are any types of waste that you throw out a lot!

This hands-on activity involves sorting through gross rubbish so make sure you ask an adult to help you.

YOU WILL NEED:

- Your bin full of rubbish
- A space large enough to sort through all this rubbish (e.g. pavement)
- Something to mark the ground with (e.g. chalk)
- Gloves

WHAT TO DO:

1. Put on your gloves to protect your hands from grossness.

2. Take pieces of rubbish out of the bin one by one and sort them into the following categories: Soft Plastic, Hard Plastic, Aluminium/Steel, Paper/Cardboard, Glass, Food/Organic and Clothes/Toys/Other.

3. Mark out a circle on the ground. This could be with chalk if you are on the pavement or rope/string if you are on the grass.

4. Compare the sizes of your piles of rubbish to decide how big each slice of the pong pie should be.

5. Mark out the slices and place your rubbish in its slice of the pong pie.

6. Take a photo or draw a picture.

7. Sort all your rubbish into the correct collection bin. After going through Waste Warrior training you might have a few other ideas of where things can go too!

8. Take off your gloves and WASH YOUR HANDS!

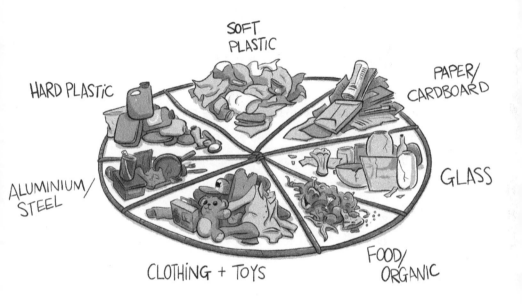

SOFT PLASTIC

HARD PLASTIC

PAPER/ CARDBOARD

ALUMINIUM/ STEEL

GLASS

CLOTHING + TOYS

FOOD/ ORGANIC

Make sure to take notes about this project in your

Garbology Lab Book.

EXTRA EXPERIMENTAL

Here are a few ideas to make your pong pie into more of an experiment so you can do some garbological research of your own. If you try any of these ideas out then be a good garbologist and make sure you write down what you did and what your results were in your <u>Garbology Lab Book</u>.

1. THE BIGGEST SLICE OF PIE

How did you divide your slices of the pie? Was it based on the amount of space the rubbish took up? That's a really good first step. Another way to calculate how big each slice should be is to weigh your waste and compare the weight of each type.

Which types of waste might take up lots of space but not weigh much? Which types of waste might weigh a lot but not take up much space? Does this change what your pong pie looks like?

2. TRACKING PIE PROGRESS

As you go through your Waste Warrior training you can create a new pong pie every time your bin gets full. This will help you to see whether there have been any changes in how much of each type of rubbish is ending up in your bin. Think about some of the reasons it might change?

Instead of making your piles into pie. What other ways could you track your progress?

3. PIE-EATING COMPETITION

No, don't *actually* eat the pie! To make this Waste Warrior journey even more fun, you could have a competition with a friend or another class to see who can reduce the amount of garbage in their weekly pie the most!

SORT IT OUT!

How do you tell the difference between

HARD PLASTIC and **SOFT PLASTIC**?

Can you scrunch it up in your hand?

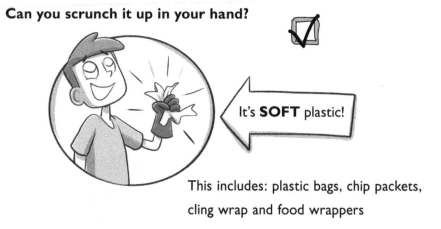

It's **SOFT** plastic!

This includes: plastic bags, chip packets, cling wrap and food wrappers

Does it keep a rigid shape?

It's **HARD** plastic!

This includes: plastic containers and bottles

REMEMBER: Some things are made of more than one type of waste! For example:

A yoghurt pot:
The lid is soft plastic because you can scrunch it up. The container is hard plastic because it has a rigid shape.

A jam jar:
The lid is metal but the container is glass.

What other types of waste are made of more than one thing?

WHAT GOES WHERE?

It can be hard to figure out what goes where, but here are some BIG BIN BASICS for you:

General Waste Wheelie Bin

This is where we put all the things that **can't** be recycled or disposed of elsewhere. We'll find out where everything that ends up in this wheelie bin goes in Chapter Two.

Recycling Wheelie Bin

This bin has some strict rules for what we can put in it. Here is a list of things we **can** fill it with:

* Paper
* Cardboard
* Glass
* Hard plastic
* Aluminium
* Steel

We will get into the gory details of recycling, and even talk about other things you can recycle even though they don't go in this bin, in Chapter Three.

You'll notice there are some slices left that don't have a bin of their own. Never fear, recruit, I haven't forgotten about them. We will be finding out what to do with those food scraps in Chapter Four. And we'll even come up with some CRAFTY things to do with your rubbish in Chapter Five.

FOUL FACTS

Do you smell something?

The smelly molecules from the rotten stuff in our bin
float through the air and into our nose. This sends
a signal to our brain, which tells us if this is a lovely
smell or a NASTY STENCH. If your bin is on the nose,
there are lots of different types of stanky molecules
that could be responsible – maybe even a mix of them.

Who's to blame?

It's only the edible stuff and plant matter (like garden
waste or old flowers) that produces this pong as it
breaks down.

So, if you want a less stinky bin, turn to Chapter Four
for all you need to know!

THE RUBBISH ROUND-UP

It's time to put your waste knowledge to the test with your first Rubbish Round-Up. If you ace the quiz you will receive a much sought after Waste Warrior Badge!

1. What are the tiny things that break down waste called?
2. What type of waste makes up the biggest slice of your garbage pie?
3. How do you tell the difference between **soft plastic** and **hard plastic**?
4. What types of rubbish go into the recycling bin?

Flip to the answers on **page 221** to see how you scored . . .

Well done! Now that you're up to speed with some bin basics, you've earnt your first Waste Warrior Badge. I hereby award you the badge for SERVICES TO MAKING PONG PIES.

Your Level One training has filled you in on the waste essentials that will come in handy for the rest of our mission. So rest up, recruit, because tomorrow we're getting up at the CRACK OF DAWN. Level Two of your training happens on my favourite day of the week – BIN DAY!

CHAPTER TWO

THE DUMP DIG

Wakey-wakey! Rise and shine, recruit. Jump out of bed, into those bin boots and meet me on the footpath – we've got a date with the GENERAL WASTE WHEELIE BIN!

Look down the street. Ah . . . what a beautiful sight. I'm not talking about the sunrise . . . although, that is kind of nice too. I'm talking about wheelie bins, as far as the eye can see. It's just magical.

Why are we here? Now that you are a Level One pong pie-making, waste-sorting whiz, we're here to snoop around and see what rubbish has ended up in all **these** bins.

Oh, you mean why are we here so early? Well, WASTE WAITS FOR NO ONE. Not even a Waste Warrior. In fact, there's already a rumble of activity across town because my favourite day of the week, bin day, is in full swing. You're about to experience bin day like you've never experienced it before.

What was your last bin day like? Let me guess . . . you walked past the wheelie bin on your way to the bus stop. Was it still full or was it already empty by then? Did you notice? Whether you noticed or not, when you came home from school at the end of the day it was most certainly EMPTY.

Voilà – it's a disappearing act! The magic of bin day.

The magician is in fact your friendly neighbourhood Garbo. And the best thing about this magic trick is it never reappears. We just keep filling the bin and it keeps being magicked away. Or does it? And does it *really* matter what we put in our general waste wheelie bins?

Looks like we've got some Level Two investigating to do. We'll be joining your rubbish on yet another journey, but this time we will be travelling further afield, all the way to the LANDFILL. If you don't know what or where that is, don't worry. All will be revealed, waste wizards!

SKILLS TO MASTER

You're about to uncover a lot of TRASHY TRUTHS that will be important to think back on when determining the fate of your waste.

In this chapter you'll learn:

- What landfill is
- How long different types of waste take to break down in landfill
- What types of waste are made by landfill
- How landfill effects the whole stinkin' planet

BRAIN STARTERS

So your bin boots have had their first taste of garbological adventure, but there's something else you need to wear if we're going to make it through this next part of our queasy quest. That's right, recruit, it's time to put your **STINKIN' THINKIN' CAP** on!

These questions will get you started on your journey to track down where your trash goes when it leaves town. Don't be afraid to think outside the box (or the bin) and get creative with your answers. The best garbologists have a guess and then do their research to see if they were right.

1. **Where do you think your rubbish goes when it disappears from the wheelie bin?**

2. **Draw a picture of the place you imagine your rubbish will go in the FUTURE.**

3. **Which slice of the pong pie do you think people throw in the general waste bin the most?**

4. **How long do you think your rubbish takes to break down?**

5. **Name something that you put in the general waste wheelie bin that could go in the recycling bin instead?**

THE **BIG** **STINK** SHRINK-DOWN

Seeing as your wheelie bins are all perfect and organised, we are going to shrink down and jump into your neighbour's reeking rubbish.

HERE WE GO!

Now that we're here in this big stinkin' wheelie bin. Let's take a look around. There's all kinds of jumbled junk in here. Plastic, paper, food scraps . . .

Waste Warrior training is not for the faint-hearted. It's a journey for all the senses.

SEE how many different kinds of things we throw away every day.

SMELL the stank of rotting rubbish. This odour comes from stinky molecules like <u>HYDROGEN SULPHIDE</u> as the waste breaks down.

TASTE . . . actually, NO! Put that down, recruit! Don't taste ANYTHING. You could pick up some nasty germs.

FEEL the vibrations . . . of a huge truck coming up the street.

HEAR the squeak of a garbage truck stopping next to the bin.

Wait . . . if we're in here . . . and the garbage truck is right there . . . then . . .

HOLD ONTO YOUR BIN BOOTS EVERYONE!

AHHHHHHHHHH!

And you thought your neighbour's bin was smelly. This truck really takes the cake! Or should I say pie?

By the looks of how full this garbage truck is we've only got a few more stops and we'll be heading to the place where things really start to get messy – LANDFILL.

We're here! Let's jump out before we get chucked out.

What a **DUMP!**

We have loads to learn from these piles of grossness.

This big stinkin' mess is called **LANDFILL**. The garbage trucks dump all of the rubbish from your bin, and all the other houses' bins, into this huge pile and it gets pushed by machinery into a big hole in the ground and squished down.

See those grass-covered hills over there? They look much more pleasant than this mountain of junk, but those aren't regular hills! Underneath are layers and layers of garbage, slowly decomposing. When this hole is full of rubbish it will be sealed and covered in dirt and grass to look like a grassy hill too.

I hope you don't think we're just going to stand here and look from afar . . . Grab a shovel and come with me.

LET'S GET GARBOLOGICAL

What is landfill? Well, to put it simply, landfill is a pit in the ground where waste gets buried. Is this where you imagined your waste went?

Now that we're up to our armpits in our whole town's trash, let's have a think about the science behind this PUTRID pit. Take a look at the diagram on the next page of the different layers that make up the landfill – there are some important garbological reasons behind these layers, which we are about to learn all about.

It looks pretty grim but there's more to landfill than meets the eye . . . or the nose! So for this garbological investigation we'll stay in shrink-down mode to get into the gory details!

THE DECOMPOSITION DIG!

Sometimes garbology is a little like PALAEONTOLOGY. We're not going digging for fossils but we ARE going to dig down into the landfill to see how it's made and what skeletons of rubbish from the past we can uncover.

This layer is five years old. What's this? A plastic bottle!

Hmm . . . it doesn't look that different to the plastic bottles we saw in your neighbour's gross garbage. Do you think they would have been better off going in the recycling bin? It's time to investigate what happens to our poorly sorted plastics.

Let's dig down further to see some older remains.

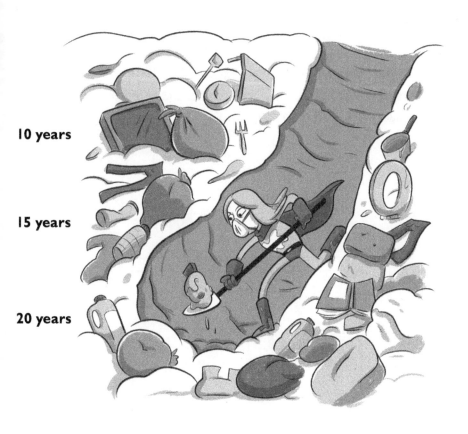

10 years

15 years

20 years

The hard plastic down here is still in one piece!

Garbologists aren't exactly sure how long it takes plastic to fully break down, but it's estimated that a plastic bottle would take hundreds of years, even up to 1000 years, to break down in landfill.

Plastic wasn't invented 1000 years ago, or even 100 years ago for that matter. This means, any plastic bottles and containers you've ever sent on a trip to the landfill probably **still** haven't broken down!

Landfill isn't designed to break down waste. It's designed to store waste. It's a place where we can brush our gross unwanted stuff under the green, grassy carpet and forget about it. That is, until a Waste Warrior shows up to unlock the secrets of the past!

It's thought that some of the things we carelessly put into landfill – like glass, plastic and metal – may **never** break down. It's sad to think of all this waste being dumped in landfill when it could have been sorted and recycled.

What happens when we wake up one day and realise landfill is FULL?

Maybe YOU could be the garbologist of the future to come up with better ways to deal with our waste, or clean up after our landfills.

Why not write some ideas down in your <u>Garbology Lab Book</u>?

FOUL FACTS

Sometimes the general waste bin is our only option.
It's important to remember that the bin is *always*
a better place for your rubbish to go than on the
ground. Litter can get washed into the gutter and end
up going into the drain and out to sea.

Now get ready for a **really** foul fact. In some parts
of the ocean, the currents have brought together so
much plastic that it has formed a floating island of
trash! The largest is called the Great Pacific Garbage
Patch with little bits of plastic spreading out for
thousands and thousands of kilometres.

Landfill isn't great, but it definitely beats THAT!

THE GOOD, THE BAD AND THE STINKY

We can't be too hard on landfill! It sometimes really is the only option we've got when it comes to managing the mountains of waste we create every day. Unless we get better at **recycling**, **reusing** and **reducing** our waste, we're still going to be piling our rubbish into this pit.

We've had a look at the things that DON'T break down in the landfill, but what about the things that DO. Get ready, recruit, in order to learn all we can, we need to delve even deeper.

Food waste and **paper** take a long, long time to break down and when they do, things get really gross. Here's the reason why . . . Because the waste is squished down and sealed on top, no air can get in. We call this an <u>ANAEROBIC ENVIRONMENT</u>. This means that lots of the microbes that break things down can't live here, but there are other microbes that do thrive in these conditions and cause your waste to make **two other** types of waste.

Phew! We've finally dug our way down to the bottom of the landfill and we're about to be swept away by one of these waste-made wastes now!

LEACHATE is a liquid that forms as the **food, paper** and other **animal** and **plant-based** waste breaks down and turns to a goo worse than bin juice. Moisture leaches down through the waste taking this goo and any other chemicals in the waste with it. The clay and plastic layers at the bottom of the landfill stop any of this getting into the ground and contaminating the groundwater. Let's see where these pipes are taking it.

THE LEACHATE DAM!

This is NOT somewhere you should go for a swim. But it **is** a place where leachate can be stored until it gets treated to make it safer.

Apart from springing a big old leachate leak that needs to be constantly cleaned up, the stinky old landfill also has a bit of a gas problem too.

The second type of landfill leftovers gets stored right over there. Let's take a look . . .

METHANE is a gas that forms from the slow anaerobic break down that also creates leachate.

BRARP!

BURP

If methane gets into the atmosphere it traps heat in, which is why it's called a <u>GREENHOUSE GAS</u>. The pipes in the landfill capture the gas in the methane recovery well and channel it into a power plant, where they burn it to make electricity. When landfills burn the methane, water vapour and CO_2 are also produced. But wait . . . Isn't CO_2 a greenhouse gas too? It sure is, recruit, and well spotted. But the warming effect of methane is much, much bigger than CO_2 (around 30 times bigger!) so it's not perfect, but it's better than letting that methane go. Sadly, not all the methane gas that a landfill makes can be captured or stopped from escaping, so our planet still cops some of it despite our best efforts.

The other thing the landfill makes is a BIG STINK. We can't blame the methane gas for this stench though because methane doesn't have a smell, it's all the pongy gases from all the rotting food waste that's the problem.

You're probably thinking, 'Enough of the bad and the stinky. What's the **good** news, Captain G?'

We can easily avoid adding to the stench, the leachate and methane problem. How? Because, recruit, we don't even need to send our food waste to landfill. You will learn all about what to do with your leftovers in Chapter Four.

And it isn't just food waste that can go on an alternative journey. We don't need to send our plastic, glass, paper, cardboard, steel or aluminium to landfill either. There are better places for a lot of our waste to go where it will cause much less of a STINK!

Right, recruits, I think it's time we got out of shrink-down mode and made a move. That bird has been giving me the evil eye ever since we arrived!

GET
HANDS-ON

MAKE A MODEL LANDFILL!

One of the best ways to understand how landfill works is
to make your own mini version. Unlike the actual landfill,
yours will be see-through so you can study all the layers.
Not everyone gets to shrink down and get their bin boots dirty
doing a dump dig, but you could use this mini landfill to show
other people where their waste goes and talk about the
waste-made waste we just braved.

All these materials are reused items that would otherwise be thrown away or are already in the bin. If you can't find these bits in the bin then think about something else you could reuse instead.

YOU WILL NEED:

- A large clear plastic bottle (you could also use a different type of clear plastic container)
- Playdough, blue tack or clay
- Plastic (e.g. food packaging)
- Straws
- Gravel, sand or small rocks
- Various small pieces of rubbish (only clean rubbish and no food waste to prevent your model getting stinky as it breaks down!)
- Soil
- A marker

WHAT TO DO:

1. Cut the top off your bottle so there is a wide opening.

2. Lay down a layer of playdough covering the bottom. This represents the clay layer.

3. Use the opening of your bottle to outline and cut out two pieces of plastic the same size.

4. Place one of your sheets of plastic on top of the playdough. This represents the first plastic layer.

5. Cut a straw to size and lay it horizontally across the plastic layer. This represents a pipe for draining leachate.

6. Add a layer of gravel. This represents the drainage layer.

7. Add all your small pieces of rubbish until you reach about 5 cm from the top of the bottle.

8. Insert your other straw vertically down the side of the rubbish so that it is sticking out the top by a few centimetres. This represents the methane recovery well.

9. Push the rubbish down to make sure it is compacted. You may want to add some more rubbish to the top after doing this.

10. Add another layer of clay and then your second piece of plastic.

11. Add a layer of soil, 1–2 cm thick, to the top and push down to compact it. Make sure the straw is still poking out the top.

12. Use a marker to label each layer on the bottle.

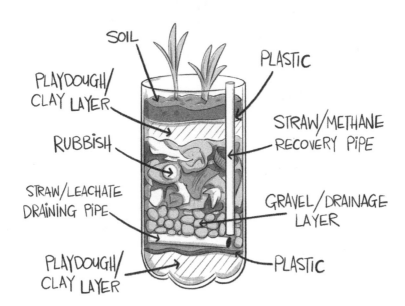

FOUL
FACTS

Garbologists don't actually know how many landfills are in Australia. There are 600 registered landfills, but it has been estimated there are another 2000 out there!

Here's the foul bit . . . We didn't always manage our landfills well, ensuring the soil and groundwater was kept safe from leachate. So there may be thousands of old pits of trash around the world leaking mega amounts of bin juice into the ground.

THE RUBBISH ROUND-UP

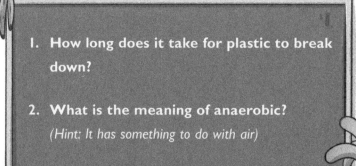

1. How long does it take for plastic to break down?

2. What is the meaning of anaerobic?
   (Hint: It has something to do with air)

3. What are the two types of waste that come out of the landfill?

Remember to turn to **page 222** to check your answers.

You've done it again! For conquering one of the grossest places for waste to end up, you've earnt your second Waste Warrior Badge! I hereby award you the badge for SURVIVING THE STINKY OLD LANDFILL.

You've learnt that landfill isn't always the best place for some of our waste to go, but we've only tracked the journey of the junk from ONE type of wheelie bin. Follow me, recruit, because the destination for your recycling is just over the hill.

Gather your strength, adjust your face mask, dry off those bin boots and let's go!

CHAPTER THREE

MEET MURF

Nice work, recruit! So far you've launched nose-first into everything from a pong pie to rotting rapids and you've excelled every squelchy step of the way. We've dug right into some of our biggest bin-based problems, but we're not just on this adventure to cop a whiff of the bad stuff, we're here to serve up some sweet-smelling solutions. That's one of the best parts of being a Waste Warrior! And that's what we'll be mastering in our Level Three training and beyond . . .

The landfill is only one possible destination for your garbage! Lots of slices of your pong pie are actually RECYCLABLE and can go into your recycling bin to head off on a completely different journey.

You can't spell recycle without CYCLE!

Remember the nature cycle from **page 35**? When things break down in nature, they provide useful nutrients for plants and microbes and other living things to eat, which keeps the cycle going. But when our rubbish ends up in landfill, the useful stuff doesn't get to be a part of a cycle.

Here's where you come in. When you **recycle** you can make a cycle of your own, where your old useless rubbish becomes new and useful again. It also means that in the future, all our paper, plastic bottles and aluminium cans don't have to be made from scratch.

So recycling is a way to make sure our waste doesn't go to waste!

The more paper we recycle, the less trees we need to cut down to make new paper.

The more plastic bottles we recycle, the less oil we need to extract from the Earth to make more plastic bottles.

The more aluminium cans we recycle, the less aluminium needs to be mined from the ground to make new cans.

SKILLS TO MASTER

Are you ready to ride the recyclable wave and SORT THIS OUT once and for all?!

In this chapter you'll learn:

- What is and isn't recyclable
- How machines sort recyclables into different types
- How recycling makes old become new again
- Why recycling helps to save the whole stinkin' planet

BRAIN STARTERS

You can *always* find out new things and new ways to give your junk a new life. Stay curious and have a go at answering these questions to get you thinking about your tricky trash as you embark on the next stage of Waste Warrior training!

1. **What was the last piece of rubbish you put in the recycling bin?**

2. **What brand-new item do you think it will become when it's recycled?**
   (You can draw this!)

3. **Are you unsure about what bits of rubbish can or can't be recycled? What are they?**

4. **How do you think all your jumbled together recyclables get sorted into different types?**

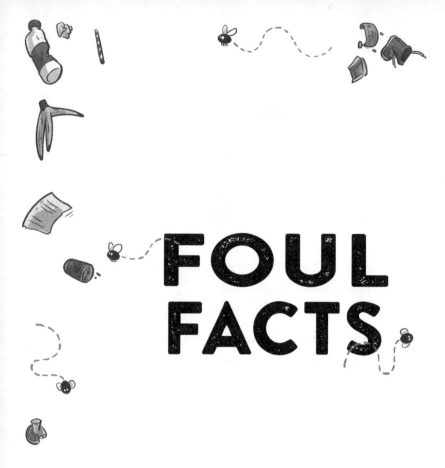

FOUL
FACTS

You've already learnt that when plastic ends up in landfill it doesn't break down. But do you know **how much** plastic ends up in landfill?

Only 9% of the plastic in our whole stinkin' planet has been recycled. So most of the world's plastic has ended up in landfill.

In Australia we use **17 BILLION** recyclable bottles and cans every year, but less than half of them end up in the recycling bin.

This is something an eco-hero like you can help to change!

THE BIG STINK SHRINK-DOWN

Since you survived the landfill, as a special treat, I wanted to introduce you to one of my best mates. Recruits, MEET MURF!

I first met Murf on my Waste Warrior training, many, many years ago – we bonded immediately over all things trash.

You see, Murf is a **big deal** when it comes to rubbish. Well, technically it's <u>MRF</u>, which stands for **Material Recovery Facility**. All our recycling gets dumped in his big mechanical belly – he's pretty handy to have around.

Hi Murf! How are you, mate? Feeling hungry? That's lucky because it's feeding time! And I've brought a fresh batch of waste cadets with me to dive headfirst into extreme recycling.

Yep, you guessed it. We're SHRINKING DOWN . . .

Take a deep breath and grab something recyclable. We're surfing this wave of waste right into the BELLY OF THE BEAST. You don't mind if I call you a beast do you, Murf?

Keep your balance, recruits, this conveyor belt is going to take us to some dangerous places.

Watch out! These waste management workers are plucking pesky stuff out of the stream . . . Seriously? Who puts a tree branch in the recycling bin?

Sometimes the surf is bumpy . . .

Sometimes it's fun . . . WEEEEEEEE!

And sometimes it's terrifying . . .
AAAAAAAAAH!

Phew, the paper pile.

The last time I was here I landed in the glass pile . . . Let me tell you, that was a rough day on the job.

Now we've got a comfy spot, let's sit back for a moment and watch **The Master Murf** at work.

THE INNER WORKINGS OF MURF

Here's how Murf works.

When the truck drops off our recycling, Murf gobbles it all up.
It goes onto a huge conveyor belt to his belly – and by belly,
I mean an AMAZING machine that sorts our paper from our
cardboard, and our glass from our plastics and metals. Once
Murf has separated all the rubbish, everything comes out the
other end as sorted piles and cube-shaped bales of recyclables,
ready to be turned into something new! We'll find out more
about how his brilliant belly does this when we take a look at
the garbology.

SORT IT OUT, OR IT GETS SPAT OUT!

Murf is a picky eater. No matter how hungry he is, he doesn't like to eat every slice of the pong pie. His favourite slices to eat are: **hard plastic, metal, paper and cardboard, and glass.** He will eat these all day, every day.

Murf doesn't always have the best table manners. If ever any **human food, garden waste, clothing or toys** find their way into his belly, he will spit them straight out.

There is one other thing you need to know about Murf – he has a love-hate relationship with plastic.

Hard plastic is a big **YES**, but **soft plastic** is a big **NO!** Even though soft plastic CAN be recycled, Murf just can't stomach the stuff. So, if it ends up in his tummy it gets spat out along with all the other non-recyclables, which then goes to the STINKIN' LANDFILL!

Turn back to the **Sort it out!** section on **page 46** to brush up on your sorting hard plastics from soft plastics skills.

TRICKY TRASH

So what happens to those bits of rubbish that can be recycled but are off Murf's menu? Well, luckily for us, Murf's belly isn't the only place where our tricky trash can be sent.

Soft plastics like chip packets, plastic wrapping and plastic bags can't go in the kerbside recycling bin because they get caught up in Murf's tummy. BUT they ARE still recyclable and can be placed in special soft plastics recycling bins, which can be found at some supermarkets.

These soft plastics get melted down, moulded and shaped into hard plastics for making park benches, play equipment and more. Clever, huh!

- What would you make?
- Where is your closest soft plastics recycling bin?

E-WASTE like **batteries, smartphones** or **gaming controllers** would also give Murf a bellyache and they contain harmful materials that shouldn't go into landfill. But our old electronics are made of plastic, **PRECIOUS METALS** and glass that CAN be recycled through special e-waste recycling programs.

If you are unsure where you should be taking these bits of trash, talk to someone at your local council or electronics store.

- What type of e-waste are you throwing away?
- Are there any recycling programs for it?

You might need to do some garbological research to find out!

MISSION RECYCLABLE!

A new truck has arrived to feed Murf, but some things have ended up in there that shouldn't be on Murf's menu.

Your mission is to surf this wave of wannabe recycling and sort all of the rubbish into three types: **Recyclable**, **Non-Recyclable** and **E-Waste**. You can use your <u>Garbology Lab Book</u> to write down your answers and then turn to **page 224** to find out how you went!

JAM JAR   MILK BOTTLE

GARDEN CLIPPINGS   APPLE CORE

GAMING CONTROLLERS   ALUMINIUM FOIL

PAPER   SMARTPHONE

BATTERIES   YOGHURT TUB

PADDLE-POP STICK   HALF-EATEN SANDWICH

CEREAL BOX   GLASS BOTTLE

SOFT DRINK CAN

LET'S GET GARBOLOGICAL

So what's the big stinkin' deal with recycling things? Sure, we want to avoid sending things to landfill, but why is it so bad to keep making things from scratch instead of making them from recycled stuff?

All our belongings have to come from somewhere (our plastic, books, phones, clothes – the list is endless) and our planet doesn't have endless supplies of all the ingredients we use to make these things. There are ingredients we can replenish and also ingredients we can run out of. As Waste Warriors we need to think about **how** we get these ingredients and whether this is tough on our poor old planet!

PART OF THE BIG STINKIN' PROBLEM: RENEWABLE VS NON-RENEWABLE

We can divide the ingredients (or RESOURCES) we use to make things into two main types:

1. RENEWABLE RESOURCES:
   Things that we can make more of and won't run out. *Note: Just because something is renewable doesn't mean we don't have to be careful with how we use it.*

2. NON-RENEWABLE RESOURCES: Things we have a limited supply of on our planet. Once we use these up, there won't be any left.

RENEW OR RUN OUT?

A great skill to have is knowing whether the things we buy, and throw away, are made from things that can be replaced or will run out (whether they are renewable or non-renewable). This helps us to see the importance of recycling things, but it also helps us make good choices when we buy things in the first place (this is something we will tackle in the final stage of your training in Chapter Five).

Try this out! Pick something from your recycling bin and ask yourself the following questions for each item.

- **What is it made of (hard plastic, glass, paper/cardboard, steel or aluminium)?**
- **Where did the ingredients used to make it come from?**
- **Do you think the ingredients used to make this are renewable or non-renewable?**

See if you can guess for each of the waste below and write your answers down in your <u>Garbology Lab Book</u>. It's okay if you're not sure, guessing is the first step to learning.

What are these things made of? Where does the main ingredient come from?

- Paper and Cardboard

  (Hint: These are made from the same resource.)
- Steel cans
- Aluminium

  (Hint: There is one word that starts with 'm' and describes both steel AND aluminium but there are differences too.)
- Plastic

  (Hint: You need to drill into the Earth to get this.)
- Glass

  (Hint: You might see this stuff on holiday.)

These are TRICKY! Turn the page and take a look at the answers!

ANSWERS:

RENEWABLE AND RECYCLABLE

Paper and cardboard are made of <u>PULPED</u> up wood from trees. Once we cut a tree down we can grow another tree so this is a **RENEWABLE RESOURCE**. But we need to be mindful of how we use trees as a resource. Trees are like the lungs of our planet, they breathe in CO_2 and breathe out <u>OXYGEN</u>. CO_2 is one of those pesky greenhouse gases that's caused our planet to come down with a case of climate change. So when it comes to keeping us alive (providing us with oxygen) and keeping our planet healthy, trees have a very important role to play.

Trees and forests are also an important habitat for all kinds of living things, so we need to be careful where our wood-based products come from to make sure we're not putting these <u>ECOSYSTEMS</u> at risk.

Some forests, called plantations, are grown with the main purpose of being cut down and replanted so the wood can be used for paper, cardboard, building materials, furniture and more.

By recycling our paper we take the pressure off our precious planet and reduce the number of trees that need to be cut down to keep up with our needs.

Do you know what your toilet paper is made from? It might be made from recycled paper . . . That would mean a few less trees get flushed down the drain!

Glass is made of sand that has been heated, melted into a liquid and then moulded into shape. Since the planet has heaps of sand and new sand is created all the time by weathering rocks, glass is technically a renewable resource. But it's much easier and takes far less energy to make more glass by recycling it than by making it from scratch.

Be careful though, because not all glass can be melted down, remoulded and recycled like glass jars and bottles can. Drinking glasses and glass windows have been specially heat-treated so they are safe for us to use, which means they aren't so easy to melt down and recycle.

NON-RENEWABLE BUT RECYCLABLE

Steel and aluminium are both <u>METAL</u>.

Steel is made up of a mixture of things (including the metal <u>IRON</u>). The ingredients used to make steel are mined from the ground. Once these resources are taken out of the ground, they can't be regrown like trees and if they all get used up, that's it! So recycling is a great way to reduce the risk of us running out.

Aluminium is a metal that comes from <u>BAUXITE</u>, which is mined from the ground too. This bauxite needs to go through a long process that uses a lot of energy to extract the aluminium that gets turned into cans and foil. Recycling aluminium and turning it into new stuff actually uses a whole lot less time and energy than getting it by mining and <u>REFINING</u> bauxite. That's lucky because we only have a limited amount of bauxite, but we can recycle aluminium over and over and over!

So recycling aluminium is the best and EASIEST and CHEAPEST and KINDEST option for everyone, including the planet!

And finally, **plastic**. The main ingredient in plastic is <u>CRUDE</u> <u>OIL</u>. This black gooey stuff is formed over millions of years from tiny animals and plants in the ocean that died and settled at the bottom of the sea. They then got covered in layers of mud that eventually turned to rock. Fuels that form this way are called <u>FOSSIL FUELS</u>. <u>COAL</u> and <u>NATURAL GAS</u> also form from dead animals over millions of years, so they are fossil fuels too!

The only place to find these fossil fuels is to drill deep down underground.

Most of the time oil comes from onshore (land) drilling, because some places that were under the ocean millions of years ago are now on land. But around 30% of the time, we get oil from offshore (ocean) drilling.

Since it takes SOOOOOOOO long for these fuels to form, they are non-renewable. If we use them all up now, we will have to wait millions and millions of years to make more. I don't know about you, but I don't have that much time to wait!

MORE ABOUT MURF'S BELLY

Now we've filled our brains with all the facts behind why recycling is awesome, let's get back to our mate Murf and how he does his job.

While we were in shrink-down mode, riding the recyclable wave, we surfed through lots of different parts of Murf's belly. The surf turned from a torrent of jumbled recyclables at the start, into separated streams at the end. Let's take a look at how this happens . . .

It would take a long time to sort the recyclables by hand – although some hands do help along the way – but with science on his side, Murf makes pretty short work of all this sorting! Each different type of recycling has special features that the machinery can use to send it all in the right direction. Garbologists call these features their PROPERTIES.

Weight is a property!

Vibrating, rumbling screens work like sieves sending heavy things such as glass to the bottom and into a big glass pile, and light things such as paper to the top to float into the paper pile. These big sieves are called **screens** and are made of turning discs that allow things to fall through.

Magnetism is a property!

This is especially helpful for sorting different types of metal. Steel is magnetic, so your steel cans are picked up by huge magnets. But aluminium cans and foil are not magnetic, so they get flung off the conveyor belt by an EDDY CURRENT.

How light bounces off something is a property too!

Different types of hard plastics can be sorted by shining an invisible light onto them and using sensors to measure the light that bounces back. That's because different types of materials allow different types of light to pass through, absorb or reflect back. The scanners in high-tech Murfs also use sensors and computer software to help them recognise different types of recycling.

Check out the diagram on the next page that shows Murf's mechanical belly in all its glory . . .

1. Worker sorting big pieces of cardboard into a pile for recycling **(manual sorting)**. They also take out any big non-recyclables and send them to landfill. All smaller items are allowed through the first screen to fall onto the next conveyor belt.

2. Worker taking plastic bags and other non-recyclables out to go to landfill **(manual sorting)**.

3. Paper has floated to the top of the screen and heavier items (plastic, glass, aluminium and steel) have fallen through **(sorting based on weight)**.

4. Glass gets screened out and crushed **(sorting based on weight)**.

5. An eddy current creates a strong magnetic field that causes the aluminium to jump from the end of the conveyor belt into the aluminium pile **(sorting based on magnetism)**.

6. A magnet above attracts steel cans onto the conveyor belt and into the steel pile **(sorting based on magnetism)**.

7. Mixed hard plastics line. The laser light shines on the plastics and directs them into three separate piles **(optical sorting)**: 1. PET (e.g. clear soft drink bottles), 2. HDPE (e.g. opaque milk bottles) and 3. MIXED PLASTIC (e.g. yoghurt tub, margarine container, sauce bottle, shampoo bottle).

THE MANY FACES (AND BELLIES) OF MURF!

Sometimes Murf gets new tech upgrades! Some Murfs (yep — there's more than one Murf out there), have special machines that scan each piece of recycling and can tell exactly what it is just by LOOKING at it. Puffs of air then blow the recycling in the right direction.

Do you know what the Murf near you looks like? Are there any things that your Murf does and doesn't like to eat?

It's never too late to get to know your local Murf. Right, Murf?

DESIGN YOUR OWN MURF!

If you could make your very own MRF (Murf) what would it look like? Think about the questions below and draw your Murf in your Garbology Lab Book.

- What types of machinery would be in the belly of your Murf?
- How would your Murf sort all the jumbled recycling into different types?
- Does your Murf have the newest waste sorting technology?
- Maybe your Murf has technology that doesn't exist yet?
- Can your Murf recycle something that most Murfs can't such as laptops or plastic bags?

Use your imagination to create the MURF OF YOUR DREAMS!

WHAT GOES IN MUST COME OUT!

So what happens when Murf has munched all the mess?

The **glass** gets scooped up, loaded into trucks and is taken away
for recycling. Everything else ends up here at the baler before
being transported on trucks to the recycling plants.

The baler squeezes each type of recycling together to make it
into a cube-shaped block. They're packed together so tightly that
one bale of aluminium can contain thousands of cans.

And in case you were wondering, any of those non-recyclables
found along the way end up – yep, you guessed it – in landfill!

WHAT'S OLD IS NEW

When these recyclables make it to the recycling plant their **properties** come in handy again. This time to turn old into new.

Glass, steel, aluminium and each different kind of plastic all have different **melting points**. A melting point is the temperature they get heated to so they melt and any IMPURITIES can be taken out. Once the recyclables are melted they can be moulded into something new!

Paper doesn't melt so instead it gets pulped and mushed together to make new paper.

Speaking of which . . . It's time to GET HANDS-ON!

GET HANDS-ON

MAKE RECYCLED PAPER!

The paper bales that Murf makes get sent away to be recycled into brand-new paper through a process called PULPING. This is a great way to reduce the number of trees we cut down to keep up with our paper needs. Even toilet paper can be made from recycled paper!

You can't melt down glass, metal or plastic at home for some weekend recycling, but the great thing about paper recycling is you can do it on a much smaller scale with stuff from around the house. So, let's get our hands pulpy with some homemade recycling!

YOU WILL NEED:

For the frame:

- A wire coathanger
- A pair of old stockings

For the pulp:

- Scrap paper (e.g. wrapping paper, craft scraps, notepaper, paper bags or newspaper – any waste paper. But avoid using glossy pages like magazines)
- A large tub or container big enough to fit your frame in it
- Water
- A blender (if you don't have a blender you can use a spoon or mortar and pestle)
- Food colouring, petals, colourful tissue paper (optional)

How to make your frame:

1. Bend the wire coathanger into a rectangular or square shape.
2. Stretch one leg of the stockings over the coathanger so that it's completely covered.

Paper to pulp to paper again!

1. Rip your scrap paper into small pieces and place into a bowl.
2. Add water until the paper is covered and leave it overnight.
3. Place a couple of handfuls of the soggy paper into the blender and add more water than paper so the pieces are completely covered.

4. Blend until it becomes a mushy pulp. Keep adding more paper and water as you go. Continue blending until you can't see any pieces of paper or clumps.

5. Pour the pulpy water into the large tub and sink your frame slowly into the pulpy water so the fine pulp settles on top.

6. Pull the frame out of the water and shake to spread the pulp out evenly.

7. Add decorations such as petals, drops of food colouring or coloured tissue paper (optional).

8. Squeeze out excess water by pressing on the pulp.

9. Leave the frame out in the sun. Once your paper is completely dry you can peel it off the wire frame.

EXTRA
EXPERIMENTAL

To perfect your recycled paper why not experiment with different recipes by adding different types and thicknesses of paper and cardboard to the mix and changing the amount of water added.

As always, write down your results in your Garbology Lab Book to keep track.

- What can you use your homemade recycled paper for?
- Are there other things you'd like to decorate your recycled paper with?

You could make a mask!

Or a hat!

Or a card for
someone you love
that says 'I love you,
but I also love the
whole stinkin' planet
so you need to get better
at recycling'.

They'll love that!

FOUL FACTS

How many trees have YOU flushed down the toilet?

Our planet flushes around **27,000 trees** down the drain with our poos and wees every single stinkin' day as toilet paper!

But toilet paper can be made entirely of recycled paper. Recycling paper uses around half as much energy as making paper from a tree from scratch and 90% less water.

So how many times can we recycle paper? Can recycled paper be recycled again? YES! Paper can be repulped and recycled to make new paper up to **7 TIMES!** Every time paper gets pulped and recycled, the tiny fibres in it shorten and it becomes a bit weaker. New non-recycled pulp can be added with recycled paper pulp for extra strength if needed.

THE RUBBISH ROUND-UP

1. **Name something that is recyclable.**
   (Hint: Something that Murf likes to eat)

2. **Name something that is NOT recyclable.**
   (Hint: Something Murf spits out)

3. **Name one property that helps recycling get sorted by Murf's machinery?**

Remember to turn to **page 223** to check your answers.

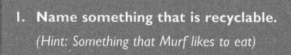

Another job well done! It looks like your recycling bin will be full
of tasty trash for Murf to gobble up, sort and squish into cubes.
You've earnt your third Waste Warrior Badge and I hereby
award you this badge for excellence in MURF SURFING!

Now that we've sorted out recycling, we've ticked a lot of
slices from our pong pie off the list: steel and aluminium, paper,
cardboard, plastic and glass. But we still need to find a place for
those leftover pieces of the putrid pie that Murf didn't polish off.

Speaking of leftovers, Level Four of your training involves all
those soggy food scraps of yours.

CHAPTER FOUR

THE FOOD WASTE FEAST

So far it's been a rubbish roller-coaster of a ride; we dug down deep into the landfill, we've surfed the recycling waste wave, and now, recruits, we're off to sink our teeth into the most delicious slice of our big stinkin' pong pie!

To earn your Level Four Waste Warrior Badge, you'll need to master the art of turning funky food waste into something fresh.

Do some of your lunch box scraps end up in landfill? You're not alone. Right now, most of the world's uneaten leftovers, peels, stalks and seeds end up in the general waste wheelie bin and find themselves rotting away in the stinky landfill.

Did you know that food waste is a big reason the landfill is stinky at all? In fact, more food waste ends up in landfill than any other type of waste on the planet. And this festering food is the main thing that causes all that **leachate** and **methane**.

But our leftovers don't have to cause such a big stinkin' problem for the planet, and I'm going to show you how. This part of our garbological adventure happens much closer to home, and much closer to dinnertime!

You're going to learn how to master this menu of mess with the power of <u>COMPOSTING</u>, so you can serve up something the planet will enjoy much more than leachate and methane.

SKILLS TO MASTER

If you can stomach this stage of your training you'll be set to make a big difference to the state of our landfill.

In this chapter you'll learn:

- What composting is
- The types of waste we can compost
- How composting compares to landfill
- The effect that food waste can have on our whole stinkin' planet

BRAIN STARTERS

We have favourite foods and foods we think are gross. But even your *least* favourite food has a part to play in this stage of your training. Food gives you the energy to go on your garbological adventures, and it powers your big stinkin' BRAIN. I hope you've had plenty to eat today because it's time for you to fire up that brain of yours and sink your teeth into these juicy questions.

We love thinking about food when we're hungry, but the scraps we leave in our lunchbox or toss out when we've had our fill are the things you'll need to think more about from now on!

1. **What food waste have you chucked in the bin recently?**

   (e.g. *it could be uneaten crusts or apple cores or soggy cereal*)

2. **How long do you think your food takes to break down if it goes to landfill?**

3. **What could you do or change to reduce how much food you throw away?**

4. **What do you think you could do with food scraps, besides throwing them in the bin?**

FOUL FACTS

Do you know where maggots come from?

Flies lay their eggs, usually on nice food waste, where they know their babies will have lots to eat when they hatch.

When fly eggs hatch, maggots come out. These maggots eat and eat and grow and grow until they form a hard shell called a <u>PUPA</u>. When they're ready, they emerge from the shell as an adult fly and the life cycle starts again!

So keep those flies away from your food scraps bin or you might get overrun with maggots. YUCK!

THE BIG STINK SHRINK-DOWN

It's that time again, Waste Warrior wannabes. We're going to take our training to the next level and get face to foul face with our FESTERING FOOD! We're going to dive into the compost heap, where all our leftovers come to party at the DECOMPOSITION disco.

The food at this shindig is something to behold! I've taken the liberty of serving up all those scraps from the food waste slice of your pong pie. You might recognise some of the things on the menu; that uneaten sandwich that came home in your lunch box, potato peels from that delicious Sunday roast, apple cores, a half eaten muesli bar, those last few bits of cereal that didn't make it to your mouth this morning, and to top it all off, a brown, mushy banana that was hiding at the bottom of your schoolbag. Deeeeeeelicious!

Now that is quite the putrid slice of pie . . . Ready to take a bite?

Yeah, I didn't think so.

Luckily for us there are lots of little critters that would love to chow down on this stuff. In fact, by the look of that fuzzy mould and the rank odour of this rotten pile, I'd say there are plenty of <u>MICROORGANISMS</u> and other critters already feasting on the food you threw away!

So what are we waiting for, let's shrink ourselves down and go
UNDERCOVER at this food waste feast. No need for the bin
boots, for this big stink shrink-down we will disguise ourselves
as WRIGGLING MAGGOTS so we can dive in and do some
detective work – totally undetected!

Watch your step. Or should I say . . . watch where you wriggle?

The food scraps bin is being emptied so we've got some menu additions coming in from above!

GUESTS OF SQUALOR

Let's meet some of the party guests enjoying the feast!

BACTERIA

These teeny-tiny dinner guests are so small
they can't be seen without a microscope.
That is, unless you're in shrink-down mode
like us. They come in many shapes and sizes,
and if you invite the good ones and
keep their party pooper cousins
out, you'll always have a
great time.

EARTHWORM

These wiggly, wriggly critters are the life of the party, forming a festive conga line as they squirm their way through the decomposition dancefloor. They're a breath of fresh air.

FUNGI

These guys sure are fun! From mushrooms that spread spores to grow more guests, to fuzzy-wuzzy mould that spreads the love across all its favourite foods. They are must-have guests at any festy feast.

You'll get the garbological lowdown on these guests once we burrow further into the science of composting. That's right, maggots – I mean, mates – it's time to get GARBOLOGICAL!

LET'S GET GARBOLOGICAL

COMPOSTING 101

Composting our food waste is much better for the environment than sending it to the stinky landfill.

You may well be wondering what the difference between landfill and composting is – either way we're putting our leftovers into the dirt to break down so it's the same, right? THINK AGAIN!

Composting is the process that breaks down food waste into compost, which is soil full of **nutrients** that plants love to grow in and little critters love to live in. It's nature's way of recycling to make FERTILISER!

In the compost bin we host a big food waste feast and invite bugs and grubs from far and wide to come along. They may not be welcome in your kitchen bin (they do tend to stink up the place), but they **are** welcome in our compost bin!

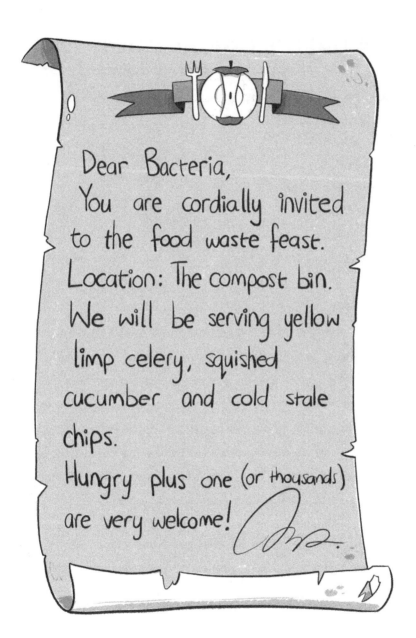

Dear Bacteria,
  You are cordially invited to the food waste feast.
Location: The compost bin.
We will be serving yellow limp celery, squished cucumber and cold stale chips.
Hungry plus one (or thousands) are very welcome!

A GARBOLOGICAL GUEST LIST

Now we will take a garbological look at those guests we saw in shrink-down mode:

BACTERIA

Bacteria are a type of microbe that are sometimes called germs and they have a bit of a bad reputation. There are lots of different kinds of bacteria,

and it's true that some bacteria can make us sick. But we can't judge **all** bacteria just because some of them are uninvited, misbehaving guests. We do always try to avoid touching gross stuff, and we always wash our hands because we do need to be careful not to let any bad bacteria in our lives, but bacteria aren't entirely bad! The world wouldn't be the same without those helpful bacteria that break things down, which is what the bacteria in the compost are doing a great job of.

Did you know that there are even **good bacteria** living in your gut, helping to break down your food? So bacteria breaks down food inside **and** outside your body – what amazing little critters!

EARTHWORMS

Unlike bacteria, earthworms aren't microscopic because they're big enough for us to see with our own eyes. Worms might make you feel a bit squirmy, but they turn our scraps into soil by eating them up and pooping out the type of nutritious, delicious soil that plants DREAM of! You can even make food feasts specifically for worms by creating a **worm farm**. Some people even collect worm wee from these farms to spray on their plants to give them a boost!

Earthworms and their insect mates are important dinner guests to include at these feasts. They are great at burrowing around, making holes through the waste and dirt, and keeping it airy so everyone at the party can breathe easy!

FUNGI

It's pronounced FUN-GEE or even FUN-GUY! It's the word for more than one FUNGUS, and these guys sure are FUN to have around. MUSHROOMS and MOULD (that green, blue or white fuzzy stuff you might have seen on your food when it's gone off) are just two types of fungi. In fact, mushrooms are the SPORE-spreading fruit of a fungi that you can't see. Fungi have long tiny tentacle-like strands called MYCELIA that they stretch out to find their food. When it comes to eating, Fungi have some pretty interesting table manners. Instead of gobbling up their food to digest it, they spit their DIGESTIVE JUICES onto their meal and break it down **outside** their body before absorbing the tiny food molecules this creates. That wouldn't be polite at your dinner table, but this is a food waste feast so it's totally cool . . . Even though it's totally gross!

WHAT!?

WHAT CAN GO IN THE COMPOST BIN?

Here's a question for you, recruit. What can we feed our gross guests? Let's check . . .

RSVP:
Dietary requirements:
Organic waste only.

What do these critters mean by ORGANIC WASTE?

Organic waste is anything that is CARBON-BASED. Anything that used to be living or is living – including the things we eat – are made of tiny parts that contain carbon and that's what our microbe-mates love to chow down on.

Let's put some menu options to the organic test!

FOOD SCRAPS

All fruits and vegies are parts of plants that are living things, so they are organic. Even the bits we don't eat – such as the seeds, stems and skin are organic. Remember, **anything** humans eat, microbes can eat too!

GARDEN CLIPPINGS

While *we* don't like to eat grass clippings and leaves, these plant parts are organic treats your hungry guests will enjoy.

PAPER AND CARDBOARD

Yep, they're organic too. What living thing is paper and cardboard made from? You guessed it – trees!

WHAT CAN'T GO IN THE COMPOST BIN?

While our dinner guests aren't fussy, there are a few things that should be left off the menu.

PLASTIC, METAL (aluminium and tin) and GLASS

The compost is no place for this trash. We've already learnt about a far better place for all this stuff – the recycling bin!

CLOTHES and TOYS

This unwanted waste is another no-go for the compost, but we will be learning what to do with this junk in Chapter Five.

MEAT and DAIRY

These are tricky. Meat and dairy are organic and compostable, but they do attract flies (who leave behind their maggot babies) and can cause a BIG STINK. If meat and dairy find their way into the party, they will make the compost overheat as they break down so it's good to avoid composting them. Try not to waste any meat and dairy foods so you don't have to throw them out!

PET POOP

Dog and cat doo-doos can contain diseases that should stay out of your garden. If you want to compost your furry friend's droppings, it's best to make a special compost heap just for that.

CITRUS PEELS and ONIONS

Peel from lemons, oranges and other citrus, as well as onions, should be left out of the compost heap because

they contain natural chemicals that can send our dinner guests packing. The last thing we want is a feast with no one around to eat it!

COMPOST vs LANDFILL

What's the big stinkin' deal? Why host a compost party at home instead of sending our food to landfill? It all comes down to the landfill being an **anaerobic** environment and the compost bin being an <u>AEROBIC</u> environment.

In landfill, when organic waste breaks down, the carbon from all the food scraps, paper waste and garden clippings ends up as part of the nasty methane gas that forms. But in the compost, the oxygen-loving microbes and worms use this carbon to make other things, like POOP, so it doesn't end up as methane. Instead, their poop makes nutrient-rich soil that can be used in the garden to grow vegies and other plants.

Those methane-making microbes aren't invited to the compost party. As long as we make sure lots of air is available to our helpful microbes, we will keep these uninvited guests away!

So security is sorted, the guest list is done and the menu is set. To invite these critters into your life so they can help you save the whole stinkin' planet, you're going to have to get your hands dirty and GET HANDS-ON!

GET HANDS-ON

MAKE A MINI COMPOSTER

You don't have to start big to get into composting. You can make your own mini feast of food waste and invite helpful critters to the party by starting small. Your mini composter is the perfect place to start and try different combinations of food waste and other ingredients to see what gets those microbes drooling. And who knows? You might end up planning a big food waste festival!

YOU WILL NEED:

- A large empty plastic bottle (from the recycling bin)
- Paper (from the recycling bin) or leaves
- Food waste
- Soil
- Water (in a spray bottle if you have one)
- An adult with a pair of scissors (if your adult doesn't come with scissors please exchange them for an adult who does)
- Patience

WHAT TO DO:

1. Cut around the top of the bottle so that you have a large opening at the top.

2. Poke some small holes in the sides of the bottle a few centimetres from the top. You may want to ask your adult to help with this step.

3. Layer your ingredients, spraying or sprinkling each layer with water (just enough to dampen it) as you go. Layer it in this order: **shredded/ripped up paper or leaves, soil, food scraps, soil,** and so on.

4. Mark the level of your ingredients with a marker so you can see whether it changes in size while it composts.

5. Well done – you've made a mini composter!

COMPOST CARE

Don't just walk away and leave your composter all alone. This little fella needs a lot of care!

• •

Give it warmth

Keep it in a warm spot for 4–6 weeks.

Give it water

Give it another spray or sprinkle of water if it looks like it's drying out.

Give it air

Give it a stir every now and then to mix the ingredients and let lots of air in.

Give it attention

Keep an eye on the mark you made to see if the level has gone down. Take a photo each day to see how it changes over time.

After all this hard work your mini composter will give you something in return . . .

Once your food waste has broken down, you'll have some nice fresh compost! You can now put it in the garden or you could poke some holes in the bottom of your bottle and plant something in it.

EXTRA EXPERIMENTAL

Here are a few ideas to make this mini composter activity into more of an experiment so you can do some garbology research of your own. If you try any of these out, then be a good garbologist and write down what you did and what your results were in your Garbology Lab Book.

1. **Battle of the composters**

   Make several mini composters, keeping all the steps the same except one to see if it makes a difference.

   For example:
   - What if you make three identical composters but put one in the dark, one in full sun and one in the shade?
   - What if you only put leaves and grass in one and fruit and vegetable scraps in another?

2. **Decomposition dig**

   Bury different items in your mini composter and dig them up at different times to see how long they take to break down.

   For example:
   - How long does it take a teabag to break down?
   - Does this change when you add more water or put your composter in a warmer place?

3. **Compost and compare**

   Cut two squares of paper, exactly the same size, out of your <u>Garbology Lab Book</u>. Write 'COMPOST ME' on one of the squares and put it in your mini composter. Dig it up every day or every few days (you decide!) and see whether it changes in shape and size. On the other square, write 'COMPARE ME'. This square will be used as a <u>CONTROL</u> so you can compare it to the square you placed in your compost.

   Each time you remove the 'COMPOST ME' square, make a note or take a picture of how much it has changed. You can even draw an outline on the comparison square and mark the day so you can see how it breaks down over time. Don't forget to bury it in the compost again when you're finished!

   You can repeat this experiment as many times as you like with different types or sizes of paper and see whether changing your compost mixture or conditions changes how quickly the paper breaks down.

4. **Build it bigger!**

   Now that you've made a mini compost bin maybe you could make a big one in the backyard, at your school or in your community that can handle even more food waste.

5. **Reduce**

   One of the best thing to do is to reduce the amount of food you throw out to start with. You can do this by eating everything on your plate, being careful not to take more food than you can eat and eating food before it goes bad. There are lots of tips for reducing other types of waste in Chapter Five.

FOUL FACTS

Did you know that food scraps make up most of the weight of the average waste wheelie bin?

Australians throw out **4.3 MILLION TONNES** of food waste every year. That's the weight of 81 Sydney Harbour Bridges! And here's the foulest fact, most of that (71 Sydney Harbour Bridges-worth of it) goes to landfill where it creates nasty methane and leachate. Imagine if we changed that by composting!

THE RUBBISH ROUND-UP

1. What is composting?

2. What items can go in the compost bin?

3. What can you do to take care of your composter?

Remember to turn to **page 225** to check your answers.

Well done, maggots! For your undercover work and dedication to decomposition, you've earnt your fourth Waste Warrior Badge.

So how are we tracking? We've got to know our recyclables from our compostables and our landfill from our Murf. We've found a planet-friendly home for pretty much everything we throw away. Surely this means you're a Waste Warrior now, right?

Well, almost. To really prove you've got what it takes, I've saved the biggest challenge for last. Take that maggot suit off, put your thinking cap on and follow me for Level Five of your training.

CHAPTER FIVE

REIMAGINE RUBBISH

We've travelled far and wide on our garbological adventure, and have ticked off lots of steaming slices of our pong pie along the way. But best of all, we've learnt what to do with our waste and the many journeys we could send it on.

Let's check out your pong pie one last time and take a look at all the rubbish we've recycled, composted and put to good use without hurting the planet!

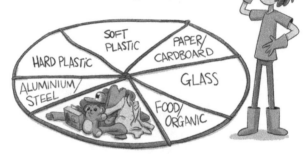

- The aluminium and steel, paper and cardboard, glass and hard plastics were gobbled up by MURF and sent off to be recycled into something new.
- The soft plastics went to a special recycling bin and will live their next life as hard plastics.
- The organic waste was composted into nutrient-rich soil.

But there's still a slice of pie we haven't touched yet! This tricky trash can't easily be recycled and composting is out of the question. So what journey will this junk go on . . .?

Don't worry, recruit, no bin boots necessary – this is the BIG STINKIN' THINKIN' chapter! In order to gain your Level Five Waste Warrior Badge all you need is your IMAGINATION. You will be working out ways to give your trash a new lease of life. You will also learn how to recognise when so called 'RUBBISH' is actually way too good to rot away in landfill or get fed into MURF's rumbling tum! Before we send all our waste off on an adventure with our friendly neighbourhood Garbo, what else can we do?

SKILLS TO MASTER

It's time to reveal four sweet skills you can use to SAVE THE WHOLE STINKIN' PLANET! Introducing the FOUR R's . . .
REPAIR, REUSE, REPURPOSE and REDUCE!

In this chapter you'll learn:
- Repairing a busted button
- Reusing a glass jar
- Repurposing some unwanted cardboard
- Reducing our impact on the whole stinkin' planet

BRAIN STARTERS

Let's see if you've already been putting the **FOUR R's** into practice!

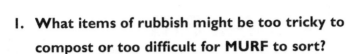

1. **What items of rubbish might be too tricky to compost or too difficult for MURF to sort?**

2. **Think of some items you've recently thrown away. Do you think you could have** <u>REUSED</u> **or found a new use (**<u>REPURPOSE</u>**) for these items? How?**

3. **Can you think of something at home that broke but got** <u>REPAIRED</u>**?**
   - **What was it?**
   - **How did it break?**
   - **How did it get fixed?**

4. **Do you own anything special that is** <u>SECOND-HAND</u>**?**
   (It could be something you wear or play with that was passed down to you by an older sibling or family member.)

THE BIG STINK SHRINK-DOWN

You've been told that room of yours is a DUMP and needs to be tidied. Well, let me tell you, I've been to plenty of dumps in my time and this really doesn't look *that* bad! But it does look like you've got a pretty big box of unwanted junk just sitting there.

Righto, recruit, before we bin it all, let's shrink down and check out this trash!

Well, well, well – where to begin? There's heaps of awesome stuff in here, but I know for a fact MURF won't be able to stomach half this junk, and putting it in the compost is a NO-GO.

Just because we've shrunk down doesn't mean our brains are tiny – let's think BIG and work out what to do with this waste.

Is this one of your t-shirts? It looks like it's in fairly good shape . . .

What else do we have? Some toys you're tired of playing with . . . Some toys that look a bit tired of playing with you!

Hmmm, some pants with a hole in them from that time you fell off your bike . . . Okay, I can see why you're not wearing *those* anymore.

Sometimes landfill is the only option, but I've got a few other ideas up my sleeve. Let's see if we can rescue some of this rubbish and give it a chance at a whole new life before we throw it out entirely!

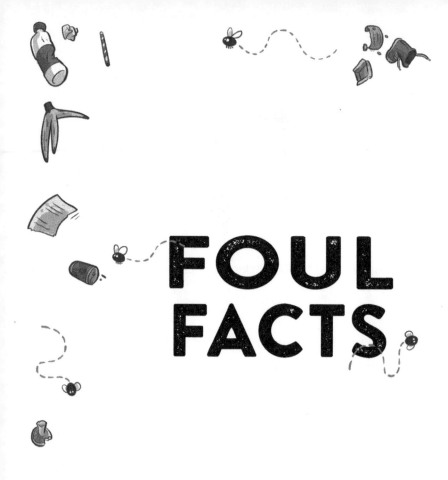

FOUL
FACTS

Did you know that your clothing might be made of plastic?

Tiny plastic fibres called <u>MICROFIBRES</u> are used in some clothing. Every time we wash these types of clothes, small bits of plastic get washed away with the laundry water and can end up in the ocean. Around **HALF A MILLION TONNES** of microfibres end up in the ocean every year!

There are lots of kinds of teeny-tiny plastics from microfibres to glitter! These are called <u>MICROPLASTICS</u>. But even tiny plastics can cause big problems for fish and other marine life who mistake them for a tasty treat and eat them.

Who knew that making careful wardrobe decisions could reduce plastic use and even save our sea creatures?!

LET'S GET
GARBOLOGICAL

Garbologists are all about asking the tricky, sticky questions and finding new and exciting solutions to our problems. That's why, for our final training mission, we're diving into the FOUR R's to learn how to stop our waste from going to waste. All the things you discover in this section can be applied to any of the rubbish in your pong pie – not just the clothes and toys.

One of the most exciting things about the FOUR R's is that they can give us ways to stop things from becoming waste in the first place. Too cool, right?

Let's break it down and take a closer look at how we can use these **FOUR R's** to reimagine our rubbish!

REPAIR

Repairing things means fixing them so you can keep using them. For example, sewing a button back onto your coat.

REUSE

Reusing means using something again instead of throwing it away. For example, using a resealable yoghurt container to store other food, pencils or even a button collection.

REPURPOSE

Repurposing means finding a whole new use for something that it didn't have before. For example, you could make a photo frame out of paddle-pop sticks!

REDUCE

Reducing means being careful about what we **buy**, what we **use** and what we **throw away** so that we use less of our planet's **resources.**

Repairing, reusing, and repurposing are all ways that we can **reduce** the amount of stuff we buy brand-new, and therefore we will end up using less of those resources! Treating your things with care so that they last longer is also a really good way to reduce our waste.

Every time you are thinking about buying something new, ask yourself these questions:

- Do I really need that?
- Could I do without it?
- Could I **repair, reuse,** or **repurpose** something I already have?
- Could I **reuse** or **repurpose** something **second-hand**?

Letting go . . .

The most courageous of eco-heroes can't always save the day, even though we try to give it our best shot! Lots of things in our world aren't made with the impact of their waste in mind, which makes a Waste Warrior's job pretty tough!

If all of the FOUR R's have been explored, and recycling or composting are out of the question, some things do only have one place left to go – yep, the landfill! But if you've used that brain of yours to rethink and reimagine your rubbish, and have explored your options, then you've already done the best you can do!

If you do end up sending the trash that was too tricky to turn into treasure to the bin, at least you know you did loads of things to ease the pressure on our awesome planet! And that makes you a hero in my books!

See I wrote it here in my <u>Garbology Lab Book</u>!

TESTING IT OUT!

Now we know all about the FOUR R's, it's time to use our imaginations and reimagine our rubbish! Brainstorming ideas is the first step to figuring out which of the FOUR R's should come into play. You might even use more than one R at the same time.

To kick off this garbological investigation on getting rid of tricky trash, let's take a closer look at clothing.

The fibres in our clothes could be made of many things, for example: cotton (from cotton plants), wool (from sheep), or manmade stuff like plastic (from oil). Lots of different types of **resources** are used to make clothing. Either way, it's not compostable and Murf certainly wouldn't want this getting caught in his teeth!

So how can the FOUR R's help us deal with our old clothes?

REPAIR: Got a hole in your pants? Perhaps you could patch it up so you can wear them again!

REUSE: Do you ever find yourself staring into a wardrobe full of clothes you never wear anymore? Maybe a younger sibling or friend would love to wear them. Giving your unwanted things to someone else who will reuse them is a great way to help save the whole stinkin' planet!

REPURPOSE: Could you turn your old clothes into a bag? Or a rag? Or could you even use your old clothes to help patch other clothes that need repairing?

REDUCE: We all need new clothes sometimes. Especially when you keep growing out of your old ones. But by following the repair, reuse and repurpose suggestions above, you are doing your part to reduce the amount of clothes being dumped in landfill.

Check out the **RETHINK AND REDUCE** section on **page 198** for more tips.

Now that we've done some thinking, it's time to do some doing! The next step is to GET HANDS-ON and make it happen. Let's tackle the first R and get REPAIRING!

GET HANDS-ON

REPAIR A BUSTED BUTTON!

What's your best move? A cartwheel? A somersault? A high kick? There's a lot of moving and manoeuvring involved in this line of work so it's understandable that a Waste Warrior could bust a shoelace, rip a cape or lose a button or two in action!

Every day there are so many different types of prangs that could leave our clothing and other stuff broken, damaged or just looking a bit worse for wear. Each bust up requires a different skill to fix things, whether it's patching a hole or gluing a crack. So to get your first fix of repairing, we're going to focus on a skill that helps mend and make all kinds of things and will ultimately help you repair your stuff and reduce your rubbish.

You guessed it, recruit, I'm talking about sewing and we'll start with those missing buttons!

This hands-on exercise involves using a sharp needle so make sure you ask your adult to help!

YOU WILL NEED:
- The piece of clothing that's missing a button
- A needle
- Thread
- Scissors
- A button

What to do:

1. Cut off a long piece of thread (30–50 cm)

2. Thread the needle. Pass one end of the thread through the eye of the needle (the tiny hole at the end). Ask your adult for help if you need it!

3. Tie a small knot in the end of your thread.

4. Line up the button hole with the place you want to attach your button and poke the end of your needle up through the fabric (from the back) at this point.

5. Pull your thread all the way through the fabric and then, approx. 0.5 cm away from your first point, push the needle all the way through the bottom of the fabric again. That's your first stitch!

6. Make another stitch to form an X shape with your first. This is your anchor point.

7. Line up your button with your X.

8. Hold the button in place and pass the needle back up through the fabric and through one of the button holes.

9. Pass the needle back down through the other button hole and into the fabric again.

10. Repeat until you run out of thread or you're happy with how secure your button is!

11. Pass the needle through the threads at the back of the fabric and tie a knot in it to make sure it won't unravel. Cut off any leftover thread.

12. You did it! Now button up and admire your handywork.

TIPS

- Be careful to keep your fingers clear of where the needle is poking through the fabric.
- This button has two holes. If your button has four holes, you might need to use more thread.
- If you make a mistake, don't worry! Mistakes are just opportunities to perfect your skills. You can always snip the thread and start again.

HOLEY TO HEROIC

Now you've got the basics of sewing down, you can use this super skill for lots of rubbish repair work. Sometimes you might even use sewing to not only **repair** your rubbish but also to **repurpose** it. When you start using some of the R's together you'll be unstoppable!

Take a look at your jumbled junk and see what you can save . . . What about that friendless, holey sock under your bed? It might be beyond repair to wear again, but if you do a bit of repair work and get creative, you could transform and REPURPOSE this sad little sock into a hilarious hand puppet!

I've done my fair share of **repairing** and **repurposing**. In fact, my precious superhero cape is the result of some serious rubbish rescue. I'm guessing you want a cape of your own, right? Well, recruit, guess what? You can! Don't be shy, come and have a closer look.

This part here? That's from a t-shirt I got as a souvenir on my first ever trip to the landfill. I loved that shirt, but it didn't fit me anymore. This bit over here? That used to be a pillow case I kept my library books in when I was studying to be a garbologist, so it's had a triple life. And this bit right here is made of some jeans I ripped while riding the biggest waste wave ever! My cape is a blanket of stitched together memories that I wear to remind me of all my garbological adventures! And because it looks cool . . . obviously!

So if you're keen for a cape of your own you don't need to go out and get a new one. Why not **reimagine** things you already have! My very first cape was a shower curtain, so you don't even need to sew to be super!

If a cape isn't your style, don't worry, I have a SUPER repurposing project for you over the page when you get EXTRA EXPERIMENTAL!

I SURVIVED THE STINKY OLD LANDFILL

EXTRA EXPERIMENTAL

Now you've mastered the skill to **repair** your rubbish, it's time to get even more hands-on and try out some projects that use the other three R's.

I've come up with a few to start you off!

REPURPOSE CARDBOARD!

Before that cereal box or cardboard tube goes into the recycling bin, why not rescue it for one last adventure, this time as a set of WASTE WARRIOR CUFFS! They'll help to hold up your rubber gloves and just generally make you look and feel ready for action!

YOU WILL NEED:

- A cardboard tube (or other waste cardboard)
- Scissors
- Decorations (It's up to you how you decorate your cuffs! Think about what you can repurpose. Buttons? Scrap paper? Bottle lids?)

WHAT TO DO:

1. Measure how long you want your cuffs to be and cut the cardboard tube to size.
2. Cut along the length of the tube to create a cuff shape with a flexible opening. If you are using a cereal box or other cardboard, cut a rectangle wide enough to wrap around your arm and then attach each side with glue or tape.
3. Decorate your cuffs! You could draw your initials or your Waste Warrior name on them.
4. If your cuffs get damaged while combating waste, never fear! You can always **recycle**, **reuse**, or **repurpose** all the parts and make a new set of super cuffs from your repurposed rubbish!

REUSE A GLASS JAR!

Jars are great containers. It's what they were made for, after all. Once you've eaten the last of the jam you could use the jar to hold ANYTHING. Well, anything that fits!

1. Wash out your empty jar and lid with warm water and remove any labels.
2. Decide what to put in your jar. Is there something you always lose and need to keep in one place? Ideas: Lego blocks, hair clips, craft supplies, toy cars. Or maybe you want a place to keep all your spare change?
3. Decorate your jar! You could paint it or make your own label and add whatever pictures and patterns you like. Draw or write the name of the treasure you'll keep inside.
4. Fill it!

RETHINK AND REDUCE!

Now, recruit, it's time to stop and rethink about the things you buy so you can **reduce** the impact your wardrobe, game collection, toy box or ANYTHING has on the whole stinkin' planet! Reducing your use and need for stuff is one of the toughest but most important skills to master when working towards your Level Five badge, which is why I've saved it for last . . .

Here are my TOP questions to ask yourself when you're thinking about getting something new:

1. Do I really need it? I mean . . . do I *really* need it?
2. Could I get this second-hand instead of new?
3. What is it made of? (Hint: Check the tag or ask your adult)
4. Could I **repair, repurpose** or **reuse** something I already have?
5. Will it **last**? How long will it last? What can I do to look after it so it lasts as long as possible?

And if you do get something new, that's awesome. Don't let it go to waste!

Wear it. Use it. Play with it.
Enjoy it!
And look after it!

When it doesn't fit anymore or it's no longer your style or is no longer fun, **repurpose** it or give it to someone else who will love it as much as you have so it gets **reused**. When it doesn't work anymore or is damaged, see if you can **repair** it. If it's beyond repair think about whether you could recycle it?

Who knew there were so many options to choose from before binning something?

Well, I did – but now you do too! At least I hope you do, recruit, because we're almost ready for a round-up . . .

FOUL FACTS

Did you know that, worldwide, we buy **ONE MILLION** plastic bottles **EVERY MINUTE!**

Most of these bottles get dumped in landfill but some find their way to the ocean. In fact, enough bottles to fill a garbage truck end up in the ocean every minute!

One solution is to recycle the plastic bottles we use. But do we even need this many plastic bottles? One great way to **reduce** the foulness of this fact is to use a drink bottle instead of buying water. And if you do have a plastic bottle you can always **reuse** it!

How long have you been reading this? How many more plastic bottles do you think have been bought in that time? TOO MANY!

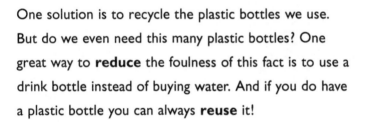

THE RUBBISH ROUND-UP

1. What are the **FOUR R's**?

2. Name something you were going to throw away that you could reuse or repurpose? How?

3. If you don't want something anymore but it's not broken or it's perfectly wearable, what should you do with it?

Remember to turn to **page 226** to check your answers.

Drumroll please! What an achievement, recruit. You've earnt your fifth Waste Warrior Badge. I hereby award you this final badge of honour, the STINK AND THINK badge for using your brain to study your bin.

That's a lot of badges you've got there, recruit. Or should I say soon-to-be Waste Warrior!

The only thing left to do is turn the page and proceed to **GRADUATION** for your official certificate and some parting words of waste wisdom.

CHAPTER SIX

GRADUATION

Phew, that was quite the garbological adventure! I hope you've learnt heaps about all our reeking rubbish and what to do with it – I know I have. But before we wrap-up this BIG STINKIN' JOURNEY, what are we going to do with all these FOUL FACTS and STINKY SKILLS we've learnt?

Let's rewind and see how much you remember. And what better way to do that than with an extra stinky QUICK-FIRE QUIZ!

You're going to have to get your brain into the right bin for this one as there are two questions from each level! Scribble your answers in your Garbology Lab Book.

Turn to **page 227** to see how you scored.

THE ULTIMATE RUBBISH ROUND-UP

1. What are the slices of your pong pie?
2. How can you sort out hard plastic from soft plastic?
3. What types of waste does the landfill make? (Hint: One gas and one liquid)
4. How long does it take for plastic to break down in landfill?
5. Which types of rubbish does Murf love to gobble up and sort for recycling?
6. What's the difference between renewable and non-renewable resources?
7. Does food waste break down quicker in the compost or in landfill?
8. What types of things eat food waste and turn it into soil?
9. What are the Four R's that help you come up with waste solutions?
10. What's one way YOU could reduce how much waste you create?

GRADUATION DAY!

You've mastered the mess with those wicked waste skills.

CHECK OUT THOSE BADGES!

CONGRATULATIONS!

It's been a gross and yet engrossing journey filled with foul stenches, putrid pits, waste waves, festy feasts. You've even made lots of awesome things along the way, including your very own Waste Warrior cuffs.

You know your stuff and you look the part, so now, recruit, I hereby name you a WASTE WARRIOR!

WHAT'S NEXT . . .?

Job done. Mess cleaned. Recycling sorted. Trash turned into treasure. All finished and ready to kick back, relax and live the luxurious life of a Waste Warrior, right?

NAH, OF COURSE NOT!

Your work has only just begun. We might have come to the end of our FIRST garbological mission in our quest to save the whole stinkin' planet, but this is really just the beginning of one **BIGGER, STINKIER JOURNEY!**

So, for one last time, let's get GARBOLOGICAL and . . .

STAY GARBOLOGICAL!

Garbologists are always thinking of new ideas to deal with our waste and are constantly researching the many different ways we can save our stinkin' planet from our stankin' waste. Now you have all this knowledge it's time to start thinking like a garbologist. Yes, you heard me . . .

YOU ARE THE GARBOLOGIST!

GET CURIOUS AND ASK QUESTIONS!

During this mission we came up with loads of answers to our quizzical questions, but I'm sure you'll have lots more.

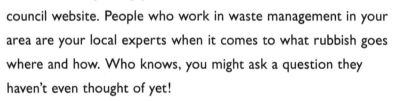

A garbologist always asks other experts for advice to find the answers to their questions.

You could ask a teacher, parent, carer or family member. You could even search the internet for more information, especially your local council website. People who work in waste management in your area are your local experts when it comes to what rubbish goes where and how. Who knows, you might ask a question they haven't even thought of yet!

Keep a note of your garbological questions in your Garbology Lab Book and make notes on your quest to dig up the answers!

GET HANDS-ON!

Design your own garbological experiments and activities.

Is there a repurposing project you'd like to perfect?
The only way to do it is to experiment!

Are you curious about how long something takes to break down in your compost heap?
Dig it up every now and then and take a look!

But most importantly . . .

DON'T DO IT ALONE!

Your next mission, should you choose to accept it, is to recruit even more Waste Warriors. Form your own TEAM TRASH and set some goals together!

Here are a few project ideas to get you started . . .

AT HOME

Make some posters to let your family know what rubbish goes in which bins. Treat them to some Waste Warrior training of their own!

And why not check out what's in your waste bin and recycling bin each week to see how your family is going. You could even track problems and progress in your <u>Garbology Lab Book</u>.

AT SCHOOL

Talk to your teachers and friends about creating a school compost heap. Think of all the food that gets half-eaten and left in lunch boxes as a nasty surprise for later. You could combine your food waste powers to make an epic compost heap! And better still, you could use the soil you produce on the school gardens.

IN YOUR COMMUNITY

Plan a team mission to pick up litter in your street or at the park. It's on a road to nowhere if you leave it there, or worse still, it could end up in the gutter and get washed into the ocean to cause problems for wildlife. Send it on a much more planet-friendly path using your Waste Warrior skills!

SO MY FRESHLY SKILLED-UP AND CLUED-IN WASTE WARRIOR, I HAND THIS MISSION OVER TO YOU.

What other ideas can you think of?

The most important thing is to start SOMEWHERE and GO FOR IT!

Put that <u>Garbology Lab Book</u> to good use and keep asking BIG STINKIN' QUESTIONS and looking for answers, even in the smelliest places!

Go forth and **SHARE THIS BOOK**, spread the word, kick up a **STINK** and get people **TALKING** about the state of our planet.

But for now, Waste Warrior, appreciate how far you've come.

Take a moment to breathe it in . . . It smells like success . . . It smells like the beginning of something big . . . It smells like . . . Whoops, sorry – I just farted!

Let's get out of here and . . .

SAVE THE WHOLE STINKIN' PLANET!

ANSWERS

Here are the answers to all the quizzical questions you've tackled throughout your training. If you didn't get them all right, that's okay! This journey through junk is all about learning something new. You can always take a look back over each level to refresh your memory.

Don't forget to make a note of all these answers in your Garbology Lab Book. You might even come up with some more questions of your own . . .

CHAPTER ONE
GET IN THE BIN!

1. What are the tiny things that break down waste called?
Microbes.

2. What type of waste makes up the biggest slice of your pong pie?
For most people this will be food waste but maybe your pong pie looks different.

3. How do you tell the difference between **soft plastic** and **hard plastic?**
Soft plastic can be scrunched up in your hand, but hard plastic keeps a rigid shape.

4. What types of rubbish go into the recycling bin?
Hard plastic, glass, paper, cardboard, steel and aluminium.

CHAPTER TWO
THE DUMP DIG

1. How long does it take for plastic to break down?
   Garbologists can't be exactly sure, but it could take up to 1000 years for plastic to break down. Any hard plastic you've sent to landfill hasn't broken down yet.

2. What is the meaning of anaerobic? *(Hint: It has something to do with air)*
   A place with no air. An anaerobic environment.

3. What are the two types of waste that come out of the landfill?
   Leachate and methane gas.

CHAPTER THREE
MEET MURF

1. Name something that is recyclable? *(Hint: Something that Murf likes to eat)*

   Your answer can be anything made from hard plastic, glass, paper, cardboard, steel, or aluminium. E-waste and soft plastic are recyclable too but Merf doesn't like to eat these, so they shouldn't go in the recycling wheelie bin!

2. Name something that is NOT recyclable? *(Hint: Something Murf spits out)*

   Your answer could be food waste, garden waste or clothing.

3. Name one property that helps recycling get sorted by Murf's machinery?

   Weight (how heavy it is), magnetism (whether it is magnetic or not) and how light bounces off the object are all properties used to sort recycling.

MISSION RECYCLABLE! ANSWERS

Serve it up! (RECYCLABLE)

These things are recyclable so chuck them in that kerbside recycling bin so Murf can enjoy them: cereal box, jam jar, aluminium foil, soft drink can, milk bottle, yoghurt tub, glass bottle, paper.

Leave it out! (NON-RECYCLABLE)

These things are non-recyclable so Murf doesn't want to see them on his plate: paddle-pop stick, half-eaten sandwich, apple core, garden clippings.

E-Waste

You will need to research where your local recycling programs are for this tricky trash: batteries, smartphone, gaming controllers.

CHAPTER FOUR

THE FOOD WASTE FEAST

1. What is composting?

    Composting is what happens when microbes, insects, worms and other living things break down food and garden waste (organic waste) to make soil that is full of nutrients that plants love to eat.

2. What items can go in the compost bin?

    ORGANIC WASTE which is anything made from a living thing. This includes food waste, garden waste and paper.

3. What can you do to take care of your composter?

    Keep it warm, keep it damp, mix it up and keep those microbes happy by giving them food and making sure you don't add any of the things they can't stomach!

CHAPTER FIVE
REIMAGINE RUBBISH

1. What are the FOUR R's?
   REPAIR, REUSE, REPURPOSE and REDUCE!

2. Name something you were going to throw away that you could reuse or repurpose? How?
   This answer is up to you! In this book we have repurposed plastic bottles for our mini composter and landfill model activities.

3. If you don't want something anymore but it's not broken or it's perfectly wearable, what should you do with it?
   Give it to a friend or family member who will love it and use it, or donate it.

CHAPTER SIX

GRADUATION

THE ULTIMATE RUBBISH ROUND-UP

1. What are the slices of your pong pie?
    Food waste, hard plastic, soft plastic, paper and cardboard, glass, metal (steel and aluminium), and other stuff (this could include tricky things like e-waste, toys and clothing).

2. How can you sort out hard plastic from soft plastic?
    Soft plastic can be scrunched up in your hand, but hard plastic keeps a rigid shape.

3. What types of waste does the landfill make? *(Hint: One gas and one liquid)*
    Methane (a gas) and leachate (a liquid).

4. How long does it take for plastic to break down in landfill?
    Garbologists can't be exactly sure, but it could take up to 1000 years for plastic to break down. Any hard plastic you've sent to landfill hasn't broken down yet.

5. Which types of rubbish does Murf love to gobble up and sort for recycling?

Hard plastic, glass, paper and cardboard, steel and aluminium.

6. What's the difference between renewable and non-renewable resource?

Renewable things can be regrown or remade when they are used. Non-renewable things cannot be replaced (or cannot be replaced in our lifetime) once they are used.

7. Does food waste break down quicker in the compost or in landfill?

Food waste breaks down quicker in compost.

8. What types of things eat food waste and turn it into soil?

Microbes and other small critters like bacteria, fungi, earthworms and insects.

9. What are the Four R's that help you come up with waste solutions?

Repair, reuse, repurpose and reduce!

10. What's one way YOU could reduce how much waste you create?

This one is up to you! Maybe you could take your drink bottle and refill it from the tap instead of buying drinks in plastic bottles. Or you could think really hard about whether you need a new game or item of clothing and decide to reuse or repair something you already have. Maybe you could find some awesome clothing that someone else has grown out of instead of buying completely new clothes.

GROSSARY

Not sure what something means? Find out everything you need to know in this GROSS but ENGROSSING glossary.

AEROBIC ENVIRONMENT

A place with plenty of air.

ANAEROBIC ENVIRONMENT

A place with no air.

BAUXITE

A type of rock in the ground that contains aluminium. This aluminium can be taken out of the bauxite to make things like foil and cans.

CARBON-BASED

Carbon atoms are tiny parts that are the key ingredients that make up all living things, including you and me. Since all living things contain these tiny parts called carbon, we describe them as carbon-based.

CARBON DIOXIDE (CO_2)

Carbon dioxide is a type of greenhouse gas. We breathe out carbon dioxide and it is also created when we use fossil fuels like petrol in our cars or coal to make electricity. Carbon dioxide gas floats up into the atmosphere and helps to trap heat from the sun in, which adds to the problem of climate change.

CLIMATE CHANGE

Climate is a pattern of weather over a long period of time (30 years or more). As human-made greenhouse gases in the atmosphere are trapping heat from the sun, this has caused the temperature of the Earth to rise. The temperature effects our weather systems (for example, rain and wind) which has caused the climate of the planet to change more quickly than living things can adapt to. Climate change threatens the ability for living things to survive into the future, including humans! See also fossil fuels.

CO_2

This is a short name for carbon dioxide.

COAL

A hard rock that is a type of fossil fuel burned to make electricity.

COMPOST/COMPOSTING

Composting is the name of the process where microbes and other critters (like insects and earthworms) eat organic waste, like food and garden waste, and poop out nutrient-rich soil also known as compost.

CONTROL

In a scientific experiment, the control is something that we don't change so we can compare it to something we do change.

CRUDE OIL

A yellowish black liquid that is a type of fossil fuel often used to make plastic or petrol.

DECOMPOSE/DECOMPOSITION

Decomposition is another word for the process where things break down into smaller and smaller parts. Microbes help to decompose our waste.

DIGESTIVE JUICES

These are chemicals that break down food into smaller parts so that the best bits (the nutrients) can be absorbed.

ECOSYSTEMS

A community of living things and the non-living things that make up their environment or habitat.

EDDY CURRENT

A circular moving electrical current that flings aluminium off the conveyor belt at the MRF.

E-WASTE

Electrical or electronic waste. This includes things like phones, computers, gaming consoles, TVs, and kitchen appliances like microwaves and fridges. E-waste contains precious metals.

FERTILISER

Something containing nutrients that gets added to the soil to make it better for growing plants.

FOSSIL FUELS

Something that can be burnt to create energy (for electricity or powering a car) that has formed over millions of years from decayed living things. Examples of fossil fuels include crude oil, coal and natural gas. When these fuels are burned, they create greenhouse gases. Fossil fuels are non-renewable.

GREENHOUSE GAS

A gas (often created by humans) that floats up into the atmosphere and traps heat from the sun so that the Earth warms up over time. Examples of greenhouse gases are carbon dioxide (CO_2) and methane. Greenhouse gases are the cause of human-made climate change and are often made by burning fossil fuels.

HDPE

A type of flexible plastic that is difficult to see through and is commonly used in milk bottles. HDPE stands for the scientific name High Density Polyethylene. See also PET and MIXED PLASTICS.

HYDROGEN SULPHIDE

A gas that smells like rotten eggs!

IMPURITY/IMPURITIES

Unwanted things that end up in something. For example, if an aluminium can ended up in a bale of steel cans, the aluminium would be an impurity when the cans get melted down.

IRON

A type of magnetic metal found in steel.

LEACHATE

The liquid waste that forms from landfill. This liquid contains water and other substances including toxic chemicals and metals that leach down through the landfill as the waste (especially food waste) slowly breaks down.

METAL

A type of material that is often shiny and hard and can be melted and moulded into different shapes. Different types of metals include iron, gold, silver, and aluminium. Some things like steel are made of a mixture of more than one metal.

METHANE

A type of greenhouse gas with no colour or smell.
This type of gas is created when things break down in an
anaerobic environment like a landfill.

MICROBES

Another word for microorganisms. These include all living
things that can't be seen with the human eye and are so
small you need a microscope to see them. There are many
different kinds of microbes including bacteria.

MICROFIBRES

Tiny threads.

MICROORGANISMS

These include all living things that can't be seen with the
human eye and are so small you need a microscope to see
them. See microbes.

MICROPLASTICS

Tiny pieces of plastic that are less than 5 mm long and
pollute the environment.

MIXED PLASTICS

A group of plastics that includes all recyclable hard plastics except PET and HDPE. Examples include shampoo bottles, margarine containers, ice cream containers and yoghurt tubs.

MOULD

A type of fungus that often looks fluffy. Sometimes white or blue mould can be found on bread.

MRF

This stands for Material Recovery Facility (or Murf!) which is where all the recycling that gets chucked into your recycling wheelie bin goes to be sorted and then sent away for recycling.

MUSHROOM

A type of fungus. The mushroom cap is like a fruit of the fungus and it contains spores.

MYCELIUM/MYCELIA

These are like the roots of fungi that spread out to find food. If there are more than one mycelium they are called mycelia.

NATURAL GAS

A fossil fuel with no smell or colour that has become trapped in rocks deep underground and is mostly made up of methane.

NON-RENEWABLE

Things that are non-renewable are not able to be replaced when we use them or are not able to be replaced in a reasonable amount of time. We have a limited supply of non-renewable materials on our planet so once we use these up, there won't be any left!

NUTRIENTS

The things in food that give organisms (living things) what they need to grow and survive.

ORGANIC

The scientific meaning of organic is anything that is living or made from things that were once living. This is not to be confused with another meaning of organic which is used to describe farming without using human-made insecticides, herbicides, fertilisers and other substances.

OXYGEN

A type of gas in the air that our body uses when we breathe in.

PALAEONTOLOGY/PALAEONTOLOGIST

Palaeontology is a field of science that studies fossils.
A palaeontologist is a scientist who studies Palaeontology.

PET

A type of clear strong plastic commonly used in soft drink and juice bottles. PET stands for the scientific name Polyethylene Terephthalate. See also HDPE and mixed plastics.

PRECIOUS METALS

Rare and valuable types of metals such as gold that are often used in electrical and electronic devices. Metals are a non-renewable material.

PROPERTIES

Traits or features that help to describe a type of material and how it behaves. These features help us tell it apart from other materials.

PULP/PULPING

Pulping is the act of turning something (paper, for example) into a mush called pulp that can be used to mould into something new.

PUPA

A stage in the life of some insects when they transform to adults. For example, a butterfly's cocoon is a pupa. If there are more than one pupa they are called pupae.

RECYCLABLE

Able to be turned into a new product.

REDUCE

To lessen or decrease the amount of something.

REFINE/REFINING

Remove/removing impurities.

RENEWABLE

Renewable things are able to be replaced when used so we don't run out (as long as we use these materials responsibly). One example of a renewable material is wood from trees. Note: Just because something is renewable doesn't mean we don't have to be careful with how we use it.

REPAIR

Another word for fix.

REPURPOSE

Use something again in a new way.

RESOURCES

Useful materials.

REUSE

Use something again.

SECOND-HAND

Something that has been used or owned by
someone else and then sold, donated or given
away to be used again.

SPORES

The tiny seed-like parts of a fungus that grow
new fungi. Fungi can make thousands and
thousands of these.

WASTE

Anything that we no longer have a use for. This usually
refers to things we throw away.

FURTHER
RESOURCES

If you want to do more research for more big stinkin' adventures then take a look at these great websites:

ABC Education

education.abc.net.au/newsandarticles/blog/-/b/2535555/25-educational-resources-to-help-kids-with-the-war-on-waste

ACT NOWaste

tccs.act.gov.au/recycling-and-waste/community/learning-tools

Department of Environment and Energy

environment.gov.au/

And if you have tricky trash questions you can't find an answer for, you can always write to your local council!

ABOUT THE AUTHOR

Lee Constable is a TV presenter, science communicator and environmentalist. As the host of *Scope*, Network Ten's science and tech show for the young and young-at-heart, Lee covers topics across the STEMM spectrum to entertain and inform her young audience on everything from sustainability to robotics to food to sport.

Lee's background is a mixed bag with a Bachelor of Science (Honours), Bachelor of Arts and a Master of Science Communication Outreach. During her Masters, Lee toured remote and regional Australia as a Questacon Science Circus presenter and founded, produced and hosted youth-run social justice and sustainability radio show and podcast, *SoapBox*. Lee is also the founder of Co-Lab: Science Meets Street Art where collaborations between scientists and street artists result in science-inspired murals that evolve live for the public.

In 2018 Lee was part of the largest ever all-female expedition to Antarctica with 80 international women in STEMM as part of the Homeward Bound leadership program. On board this voyage Lee dressed as Captain Planet, a tribute to an environmental hero of her childhood and a symbol of her hope to engage children across the world in the fight for our planet and their future.

From spending evenings as an Education Ranger with a spotlight in hand showing school groups the plants and animals of the Australian National Botanic Gardens to spending days showing kids around ACT's landfill and recycling sorting facility, there's no environment too hot, cold, dark or smelly to warrant some youth-friendly scientific communication. You can catch Lee hosting *Scope* on 10 Peach every week or find her on social media making fart jokes and talking science @Constababble.

ABOUT THE ILLUSTRATOR

James Hart grew up loving comics, cartoons and drawing. After finishing his studies he turned that passion into a full time career as an illustrator. Over the years he has worked on toy designs, animations and books for multiple clients and publishers across the world. Projects include: the popular animated series of *The Day My Butt Went Psycho*, the award-winning You Choose series, the CBCA-Notable Mr Bambuckle's Remarkables series, the thrilling Mysterious World of Cosentino series, the young adventure series D-Bot Squad and MANY titles with his favourite author Adam Wallace.

In 2018 James illustrated the Premiers' Reading Challenge posters in Victoria. 2019 sees the release of his new book series, Cowboy and Birdbrain, that he illustrated and co-created with Adam Wallace.

When James isn't drawing he can be found being a dad and husband, watching movies and cartoons, listening to music, gardening, reading and writing.

A NOTE ABOUT THE BOOK

To ensure we decreased our carbon footprint for the production of this book, it was printed locally in Australia by Griffin Press.

Griffin Press ensures all waste paper, cardboard, plastic and aluminium is 100% recycled. They have been working on reducing their company waste to landfill and it is now down 17.5% year on year. All paper and board purchased by Griffin is 100% FSC certified.

The Forest Stewardship Council (FSC) is an international organisation that promotes responsible management of the world's forest. It does this by setting standards on forest products, along with certifying and labelling them as eco-friendly.

This book has a durable cover that is designed to last. Keep it, share it and pass it on. To recycle, just take off the front and back cover and put the book in a paper recycling bin. The whole stinkin' planet will thank you for it!

ACKNOWLEDGEMENTS

I would like to thank the passionate and knowledgeable eco-heroes and science educators Shannan, Justine, Marie and Ingrid who gave me encouragement and useful feedback on my first draft of this big stinkin' journey. I would also like to thank my partner, Jason, who is the best sidekick a Waste Warrior could hope for and has always encouraged me to go on big stinkin' adventures like writing this book.